AF262601

Cézanne at the Whitworth

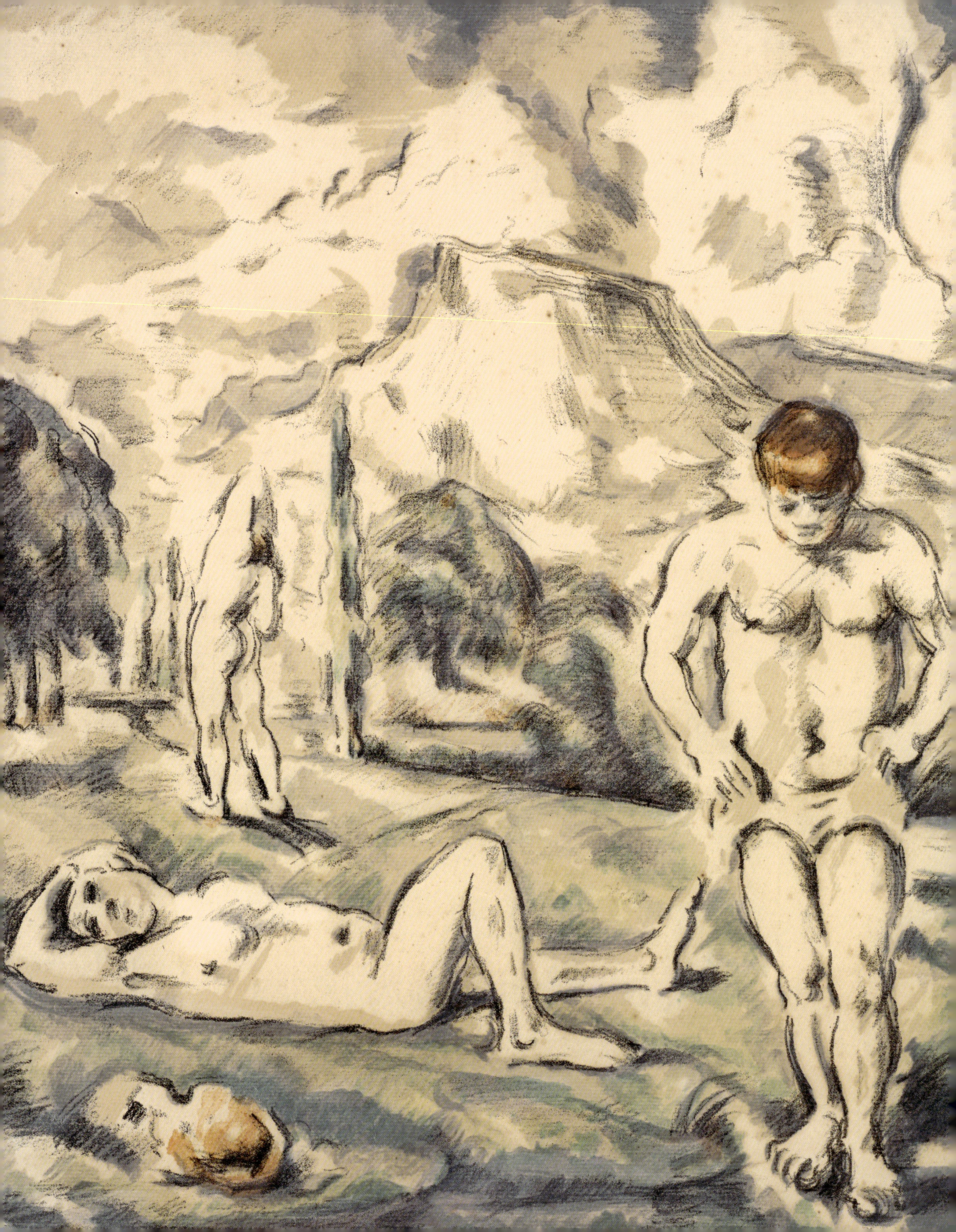

The Karsten Schubert Bequest

# Cézanne at the Whitworth

Ridinghouse | the Whitworth

# Contents

# Preface

The Whitworth at the University of Manchester occupies a very special place in the cultural ecology of the United Kingdom. Its wide and varied collections are testament to the manner in which they have been accumulated over time, not as a complete art historical survey but made with care and diligence by individuals with the particularity of their passions and the specificity of their scholarship. In the spirit of its nineteenth-century origins, the Whitworth is a finely crafted mechanism designed to celebrate creativity and knowledge with social purpose.

The joy the Whitworth gives to many is derived from the generosity of those individuals who contribute to this larger endeavour. This publication has been produced as a companion to the exhibition *Cézanne at the Whitworth*, in honour of the extraordinary collection of drawings and prints by Paul Cézanne that has been gifted and placed on long-term loan to the Whitworth by the gallerist, collector, author and publisher Karsten Schubert.

This act of generosity means that the Whitworth now holds the best collection of Cézanne works on paper in the UK, including a version of every print produced by the artist. These works will significantly expand the research potential of the Whitworth's important collection of late nineteenth-century French and Dutch drawings by artists including Van Gogh, Seurat, Gauguin and Pissarro – whose portrait of Cézanne is featured herein.

Cézanne is widely considered to be one of the most influential artists of the Western canon, described by both Matisse and Picasso as 'the father of us all'. Indeed, even amid the complexities of an expanded global art history he is still regarded as a canonical figure for the acuity of his visual literacy and devotion of his craft.

In producing this exhibition and book, Karsten brought together many people through his love and dedication for the subject. I would like to thank all those who collaborated in this endeavour and in particular the friends who have shown equal passion for the project, including Thomas Dane, Ivor Braka, Tom Rowland and Maria Balshaw; the Art Fund and those who have kindly sponsored the production of this book; and my colleagues Mary Griffiths, Leanne Green, Samantha Lackey and Olga Gribben at the Whitworth for developing and delivering the exhibition with great sensitivity. I would also like to express huge gratitude to Ridinghouse Publisher Sophie Kullmann for executing Karsten's vision for the book, designer Mark Thomson for the book design, and the authors and contributors Elizabeth Cowling, Yuval Etgar, Christopher Lloyd, Rosalind McKever, Richard Shone, Richard Thomson, Colin Wiggins and Edward Wouk.

Finally, I would like to pay tribute to Karsten Schubert for his contribution to the Whitworth and to the world of art as a whole.

Alistair Hudson
Director, The Whitworth, November 2019

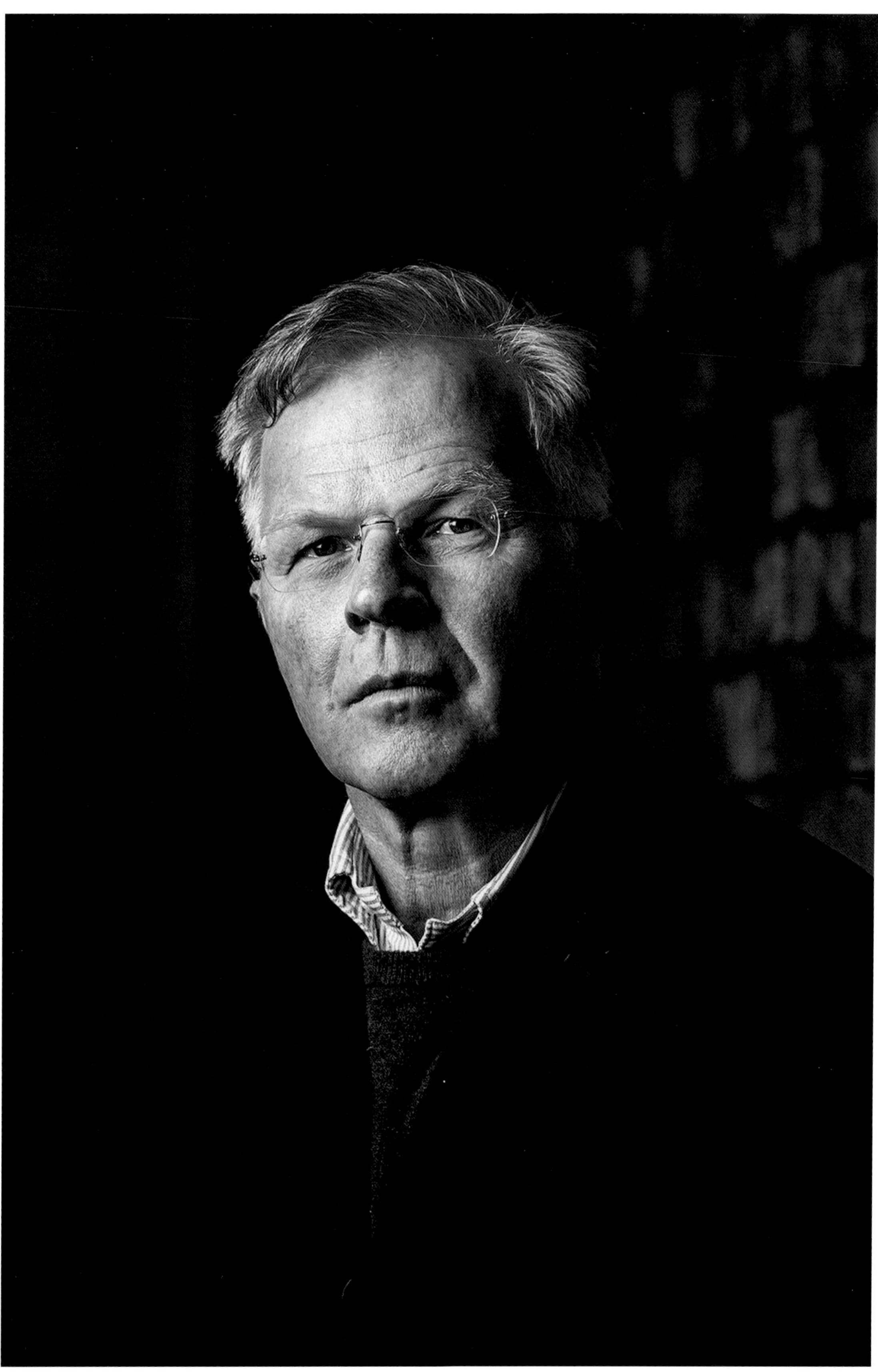

Karsten Schubert, 2017

# Karsten Schubert, Collector

Richard Shone

Most museums and galleries in Britain, particularly those attached to universities, have benefited from gifts and bequests from private collectors. Indeed, many would hardly be worth much attention without such generosity. The Whitworth is a tremendous patchwork of gifts alongside its own acquisitions; its eclectic holdings are part of its immense attraction. In the 1920s, for example, a great bequest of prints from William Sharp Ogden upped the gallery's profile; later, the collection of works by Walter Sickert given by his model and friend Cicely Hey, and, more recently, a number of pieces from the Karpidas Foundation, immeasurably boosted the contemporary collection.

Most gifts and bequests come from people with some connection to the museum or the geographical area in which it lies. This, however, is not the case with the Whitworth's latest outstanding benefaction: Karsten Schubert's collection of works on paper by Paul Cézanne and other artists. The accumulation of this group of works had begun early in the new century and took more definite shape following a visit Schubert paid to the Whitworth and subsequent talks with its then director, Maria Balshaw. The idea of the gift became a project that occupied Schubert in his last years.

Karsten Schubert was born in Berlin in 1961 and had a classic German education until he left the Humboldt University, without taking a degree, and went to work for the art dealer Michael Werner in Cologne. He paid visits to Italy and France, but after being lured by a friend to travel to England he immediately wished to live and work there. He mastered English rapidly and soon smoothed away any noticeable accent. As the years passed, he started to forget German and would even speak in English to waiters and hotel receptionists, for example, when he visited Germany. I cannot remember him reading any German literature; he was not at all keen on German music; and German art from before the postwar period had little attraction for him (save Max Beckmann). As the years passed he often travelled to Germany but treated his visits there simply as business and not as returns to the country of his birth and family. His anglicisation happened very fast.

In London he at first worked for Nicholas Logsdail at the pioneering Lisson Gallery and became familiar with the work of young British artists such as Richard Wentworth, Bill Woodrow and Richard Deacon. In 1986, with the backing of the dealer Richard Salmon, he opened his first gallery in Charlotte Street, in a cosmopolitan district once full of artists' studios (John Constable's former home and studio had been across the road until the building was demolished in the 1960s, later making way for Saatchi & Saatchi). Sculpture by Alison Wilding constituted the first of a busy, varied, international programme of shows. New graduates from Goldsmiths College – the future Young British Artists – mingled with German and American artists such as Ed Ruscha, Martin Kippenberger, Gerhard Richter and Christopher Wool. Older artists were not neglected: Rodrigo Moynihan, Bob Law and Wayne Thiebaud had shows at the gallery too.

Karsten became widely known as a dealer in contemporary art, but as a private collector his tastes were conservative. While he enjoyed aspects of British literary culture (he loved Anthony Trollope's *The Way We Live Now*, 1875, for example), Honoré de Balzac and Émile Zola were more appealing. He was not, in the main, enamoured of British art. To him the Pre-Raphaelites were of no consequence; J.M.W. Turner was absurdly romantic and colourful. It was not until one reached Lucian Freud and Frank Auerbach – both artists, like Schubert, born in Berlin – that he became enthusiastic. He began to amass a considerable collection of Freud's etchings, something that surprised and even dismayed some of his friends. Meanwhile, his real leap into contemporary British culture and society was with the YBAs. The formalist qualities in work by Rachel Whiteread and Michael Landy were substantially part of their appeal for Karsten. He was much less sure of himself over the full experience of content, and narrative and obvious social comment were not for him (thus, in complete contrast, he owned good pieces by Carl Andre, Dan Flavin and Donald Judd, which remained in his personal collection). When he came to deal in the work of Bridget Riley, whose career he helped to relaunch in the later 1990s, he was completely comfortable with her abstraction, although not immune to its suggestive, allusive moods.

It was through Riley that Karsten came to a deeper understanding of the work of Cézanne (and later of Piet Mondrian). But in the early years, when I got to know him, first editions of modern writers were his big thing: Wyndham Lewis, with jackets designed by the author; James Joyce (an immaculate early *Ulysses*); Evelyn Waugh (a great favourite, especially *Scoop*,

1938, the last book he was rereading before his death); and, later, Marcel
Proust. His bibliophilia seemed to belong to the side of him that also loved
Roman bronzes and stone heads. The most impressive of these was the third-
century head of a man – possibly a provincial governor or bullish centurion –
that was purchased at the sale of the collection of David Sylvester. At one point
he pursued copies of Old Master works by well-known artists; at another
moment small, beautiful paintings by Josef Albers hung in his bedroom.
And there was a highly characteristic late drawing by Picasso and an earlier
one from his neoclassical period. He became extremely knowledgeable
about Picasso and amassed hundreds of books and catalogues about the artist.
So too with Cézanne, about whom he also wrote several scholarly pieces for
*The Burlington Magazine*.

Karsten loved his moveable feast, researching his latest acquisitions and
showing objects to his friends. But he could suddenly tire of certain things,
and off they went into storage or were sold, one interest replacing another.
He could be quite ruthless and was not in the least sentimental. Nor was he
a showy collector: the late Picasso hung from a nail in a bookshelf; the large
Cézanne *Bathers* print leant against a corridor wall, perched on some boxes.
Although Karsten lived alone, I never had the impression he was lonely –
he was always fully occupied and his telephone was in constant use – but I do
know that his pictures and objects bolstered his sense of well-being, of having
made something of his life. Now he is gone, I am reminded of that affecting
description of Cardinal Mazarin – as recorded by a fellow collector, the
Comte de Brienne – shuffling along his stupendous picture gallery, mutter-
ing: 'All this must be left behind! . . . What trouble I have taken to acquire
these things! Can I abandon them without regret? I shall never see them again
where I am going.' Fortunately, Karsten ensured that many of his possessions
would lead another life after him, contented by the knowledge of other
people's enjoyment in the years to come.

# Crossing the Second Cliff Edge:
# Towards a New Topography of Cézanne's Works on Paper
*A Conversation with Karsten Schubert*

Yuval Etgar

It is now some years since I detected how many were the false beliefs that
I had from my earliest youth admitted as true, and how doubtful was everything I had since constructed on this basis; and from that time I was convinced
that I must once for all seriously undertake to rid myself of all the opinions
which I had formerly accepted, and commence to build anew from the
foundation, if I wanted to establish any firm and permanent structure...

René Descartes, *Meditations on First Philosophy*, 1641

Karsten Schubert (1961–2019) was an art dealer, collector, writer and publisher. In 2017 he began a process of bequeathing parts of his private collection to the Whitworth Art Gallery in Manchester. The first donation comprised more than 30 collages by the contemporary artist John Stezaker, which led to a solo exhibition of the artist later that same year. In April 2019 a second portion of works arrived at the Whitworth from Schubert's collection, this time including five drawings, four etchings and three lithographs by Paul Cézanne (1839–1906). The exhibition *Cézanne at the Whitworth* (24 August 2019 to 1 March 2020) celebrates this important donation by presenting the Cézannes alongside a series of commissioned works by the artist Michael Landy, which were produced in response to Cézanne's drawings and will join the Whitworth collection as well. Additional works by artists Alison Wilding, Rachel Whiteread, Richard Long, Lucian Freud and Richard Wentworth, among others, will complete the bequest. I met with Karsten (30 April 2019) days after the Cézannes left his home in London for the Whitworth.


Yuval Etgar: *Is it okay if we begin at the end?*
Karsten Schubert: Sure, we can try that.


*How did your relationship with the Whitworth come about?*
There are different reasons why a person builds a relationship with an institution. For me, the Whitworth is a great example of an ambitious, forward-thinking university gallery, which is a rarity in the UK, particularly if you compare these kinds of institutions with their equivalents in the United States – places like the Princeton University Art Museum or, in our context, the Yale Center for British Art. This is, of course, much thanks to the revolutionary work that Maria Balshaw did for the Whitworth during her time as director (2006–17), including overseeing the successful extension to the building and consistently developing a strong network of supporters and partners. But above all, what a university gallery means to me, personally, is a collection dedicated first and foremost to students, academics and curators, so that they can get close to the objects that they study or research. I think it's vital that you don't end up training new art professionals and scholars whose relationship to artefacts is based on slide presentations and digital images on a computer screen.

*I can't help but notice that, except for Cézanne, all of the artists whose work you've chosen to donate to the Whitworth are British. This is partly representative of your own collection, but not entirely. Is there a reason behind this decision?*

The Cézannes were always the historical exception for me. With the rest, it's really about knowing the artists – working with them and being close to some of them. I worked with Rachel Whiteread for six years, and with Alison Wilding and Michael Landy for over 30. I believe in long-term, intimate relationships as a condition for the kind of work I do. They enable me to be at once a dealer, publisher, collector and curator – and, most of the time, none of the above. A kind of 'halfway art house', I suppose you could call it.

*You described Cézanne as the exception to this equation. How so?*
Cézanne always posed a problem for me. That's why I never managed to let go of him. On the contrary, the obsession seems only to be getting worse with time. I bought my first Cézanne at Galerie Kornfeld, the Swiss auction house in Bern, around 1983 or 1984. I did it out of sheer curiosity, not connoisseurship. It was a small work on paper, a kind of modern version of *Olympia* with a little portrait of Madame Cézanne on the back. The links between the two remained unexplained; the dating too was difficult to confirm. I decided that I wanted to learn about the work and put things in context, so I brought the piece back to London with me and started reading and spending time going to see other works by Cézanne in public galleries. By then, London already offered quite a few good collections if you were interested in Cézanne: the Courtauld Institute, the British Museum and the National Gallery were of course the main places. I also started travelling after Cézanne, to see the major shows that came about every five years or so: Basel (1989), Philadelphia (1989, 1996, 2007), Washington DC (2006), Budapest (2012–13). One of the best companions I found for these journeys was Bridget Riley, who's been deeply invested in Cézanne's work from an early age, and her own practice is very much inspired by him. It's wonderful to hear her speak about him, or to look at her diagonally oriented works from the 1980s and see how much they correspond with his diagonal compositions, his experiments with colours. There really is a beautiful link there.

*You mentioned that Cézanne had always posed a problem for you. So far it doesn't sound like that to me.*
Well, my problem was not with the work itself so much as it was with the scholarship that surrounded it, and still does to some degree. For a long time there's been a very clear narrative in this field, based on a distinction between Cézanne's oil paintings and his works on paper. And within the latter category, once more, between drawings and watercolours. Accordingly, three, maybe four individuals assumed the authority for these enterprises over time. The most notable of course is John Rewald, whose catalogue raisonné of

paintings was only formally published in 1996, two years after his death. Rewald was really the axis of this field for a good half a century. Then there was Lionello Venturi, who had already published a watercolours catalogue raisonné in 1944: far too early for anyone to have sufficient information at hand, so the book is really a limited resource. Finally came André Chappuis, who took it upon himself to sort more than a thousand drawings left behind by Cézanne. Admittedly, the works had very little information [attached to them], no dates, and a marginal market. Chappuis's project climaxed with the publication of his catalogue raisonné of drawings in 1973. But while Rewald's scholarship remains hugely constructive and instrumental today, Chappuis, although fairly complete in his records, was an enthusiast rather than a scholar, and his legacy remains as such. He bought 130 sheets of drawings in 1938 and became the second-largest collector of Cézanne drawings overnight, surpassed only by the Kunstmuseum Basel, which holds some 154 sheets of paper in its Kupferstichkabinett (prints and drawings department), with 79 of these including a significant drawing on the verso too. His commentary, in turn, went undisputed for decades, even though it was founded to a large extent on pure intuition, with no backing. This was the power balance in the field for a very long time, until something started shifting with the first cliff-edge moment around 1977. But even so, the story of Cézanne was seen as a done deal, and that sentiment persisted even many years later, because there were no alternatives. It's a classic twentieth-century patriarchal narrative – I wrote a lengthy article on this subject for *The Burlington Magazine* in 2006.

*What do you mean by 'the first cliff-edge moment'?*
Well, 1977 was the year that William Rubin curated his famous Cézanne show at MoMA, focusing for the first time on the 'late works' from 1895 to 1906. This was the first big exhibition dedicated to the artist in New York since the Met had their show in 1952 – which, by the way, Rubin had experienced while a doctoral candidate at Columbia University, working under the supervision of Meyer Schapiro. According to Rubin, he was already very critical back then of the way Cézanne was understood. Anyway, Rubin's show at MoMA became a subtle but controversial reaction to the traditional narrative. He believed that the late work was being shown inadequately: in too little depth for the questions of its character, style and importance to be studied. He said very little but presented a huge number of works, trying to offer the public an experience that was like entering a repository of works, including oils, watercolours and drawings, with very little distinction or hierarchy between them. I don't think anybody took Rubin's argument

seriously at the time, but, in hindsight, somebody needed to start working against Cézanne, if you know what I mean.

*To deconstruct him?*
Yes, if you like. Or simply to follow his lead and always look at the work as if for the first time.

*I assume that by speaking of 'the first cliff-edge moment', you must have a second one in mind.*
Well, I want to think that we're experiencing the second one today. That we now realise that the more we learnt about Cézanne, the less we understood him; and the less we challenged the narratives that were passed on to us. This is true, above all, when you think of the works on paper, and particularly the drawings. It's a territory that still requires a huge amount of work, and collaboration between institutions, private collectors and scholars.

Cézanne didn't regard his drawings in the same way that he did his paintings. They were personal, experimental. He didn't exhibit them during his lifetime, nor did he date them. Consequently, as I've already mentioned, commentary on the subject was very limited until quite late in the day. But this is perhaps a good thing; there's so much work being done today – most recently by the Kunstmuseum Basel, but also in Karlsruhe by the Staatliche Kunsthalle, and the Budapest Museum of Fine Arts and elsewhere – and it's precisely for this reason that I think that the works on paper should be made available to as many scholars as possible. They should be made public.

*In that respect, we now have another hugely important resource available to us: the new online catalogue raisonné, which Walter Feilchenfeldt, Jayne Warman and David Nash initiated.*
Indeed. It's a fantastic enterprise: an open, evolving and free source of knowledge that can be updated and debated.

*I wanted to return to the question of authority that you started talking about earlier. When I asked you about the nature of the Cézanne problem, you said there were initially four scholars at the root of Cézanne's art history, but then you named only three. Who was the fourth?*
To me, Roger Fry is the fourth. But I'm fond of his writing, so I often have a hard time criticising him. I find his book *Cézanne: A Study of his Development*, which came out as early as 1927, still so relevant today, precisely because it's invested in the question of development and process rather than categorical observations. But Fry too is still trapped within the modernist project.

That is now finally tipping into history, and this means that for the first time there's a real opportunity to look, for example, at the works on paper as an equally important part of Cézanne's legacy: as a portion of his practice that enables us to explore what is incomplete, what is truly experimental and what is private in his art. It's precisely this kind of politics that is ironically late in entering the discipline of art history (I say ironically because it's usually the first to enter the discipline of art), but it absolutely must become part of it.

*This makes me think of one of the works in your collection on display in the Whitworth exhibition (cat.12). It includes four different studies: a small portrait of Paul Cézanne (Cézanne's son), a bather, a copy of a head after Rubens and, on the opposite side, a landscape too. The various elements have been dated – with the best available knowledge, at least – across a span of three years, from 1880 to 1883, which is difficult to believe and confirms much of your criticism. Nevertheless, this incredibly rich document bears witness to Cézanne's work, his private life, the influences that formed his practice and style, and the landscapes that captured and shaped his way of seeing the world – all residing on a single sheet of paper that measures no more than 22 by 12.5 centimetres.*

Exactly! It's works like this that I hope can make one see Cézanne in a completely new light, and maybe encourage new premises for an irreverent kind of scholarship: one that crosses the cliff edge, perhaps because it's no longer bound by Eurocentric conventions, or because it's interested in gender politics or in geography – or anything else, as long as it's vital and truly engaged.

It's a strange thought, that our perspective is privileged because it has distance, but we have been doing this with the Old Masters for a long time now. And while some consider such scholarship to be sacrilege, it's also inevitable: a necessary openness to give these pictures their freedom back, a freedom they might not have enjoyed for the longest of times. That's really exciting in my view. And you know, drawings have an ability that oils rarely do: they're more open, less committed to display, more conducive to contemplation. That's what I hope the show at the Whitworth will provoke; I like the idea that people might look at these cherished works and see them differently. It's important for Cézanne and for us that we change the way we see his work. It won't stop making him important, or historical or canonical, but it'll extend his reach to a broader stage. And, of course, it will make his work even more humane; it will emphasise the great humanism in it, give it room to grow.

following pages:
Detail of cat.25:
Michael Landy, *Untitled (After Cézanne's 'Large Bathers' at the National Gallery, London)*, 2010

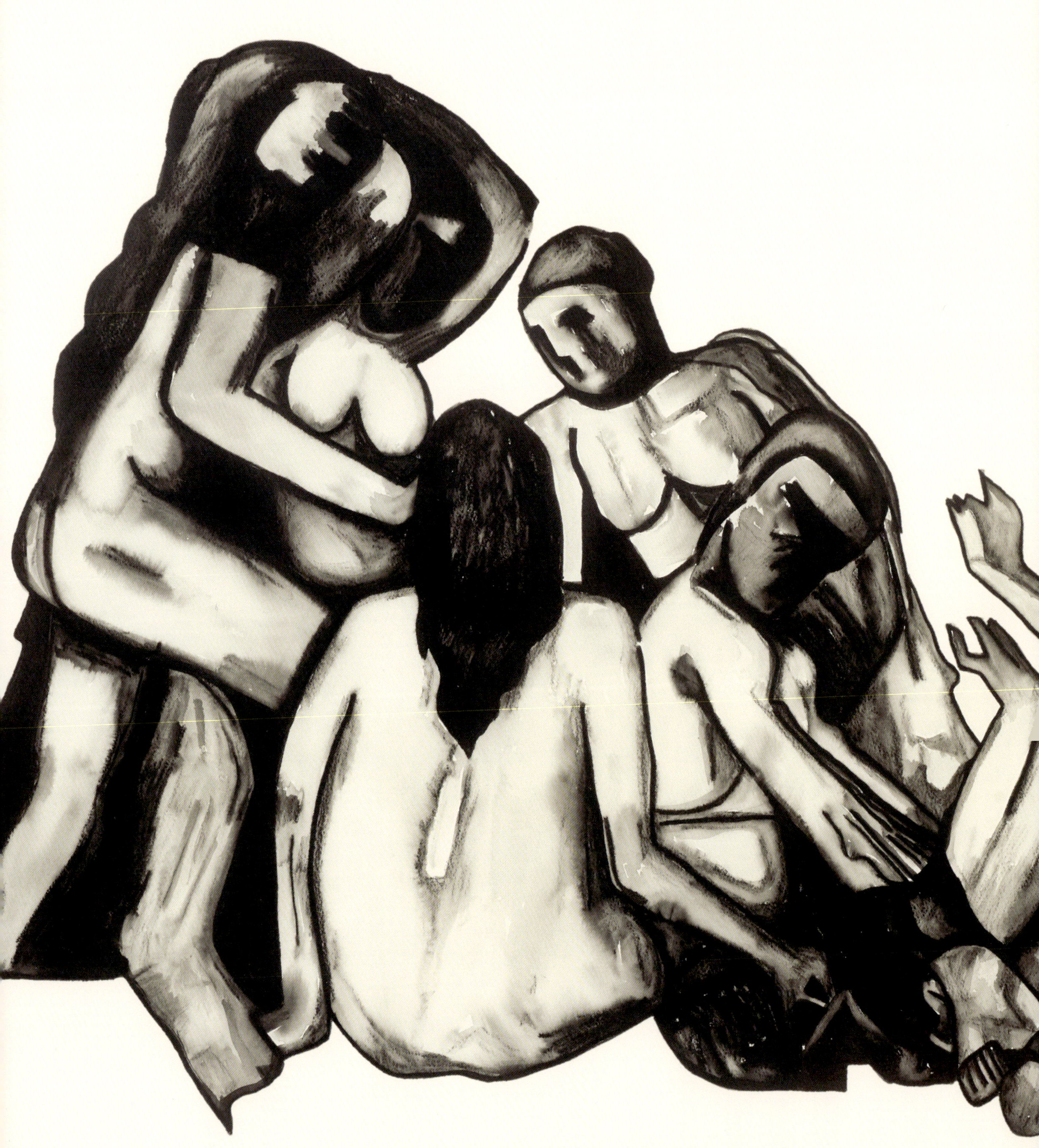

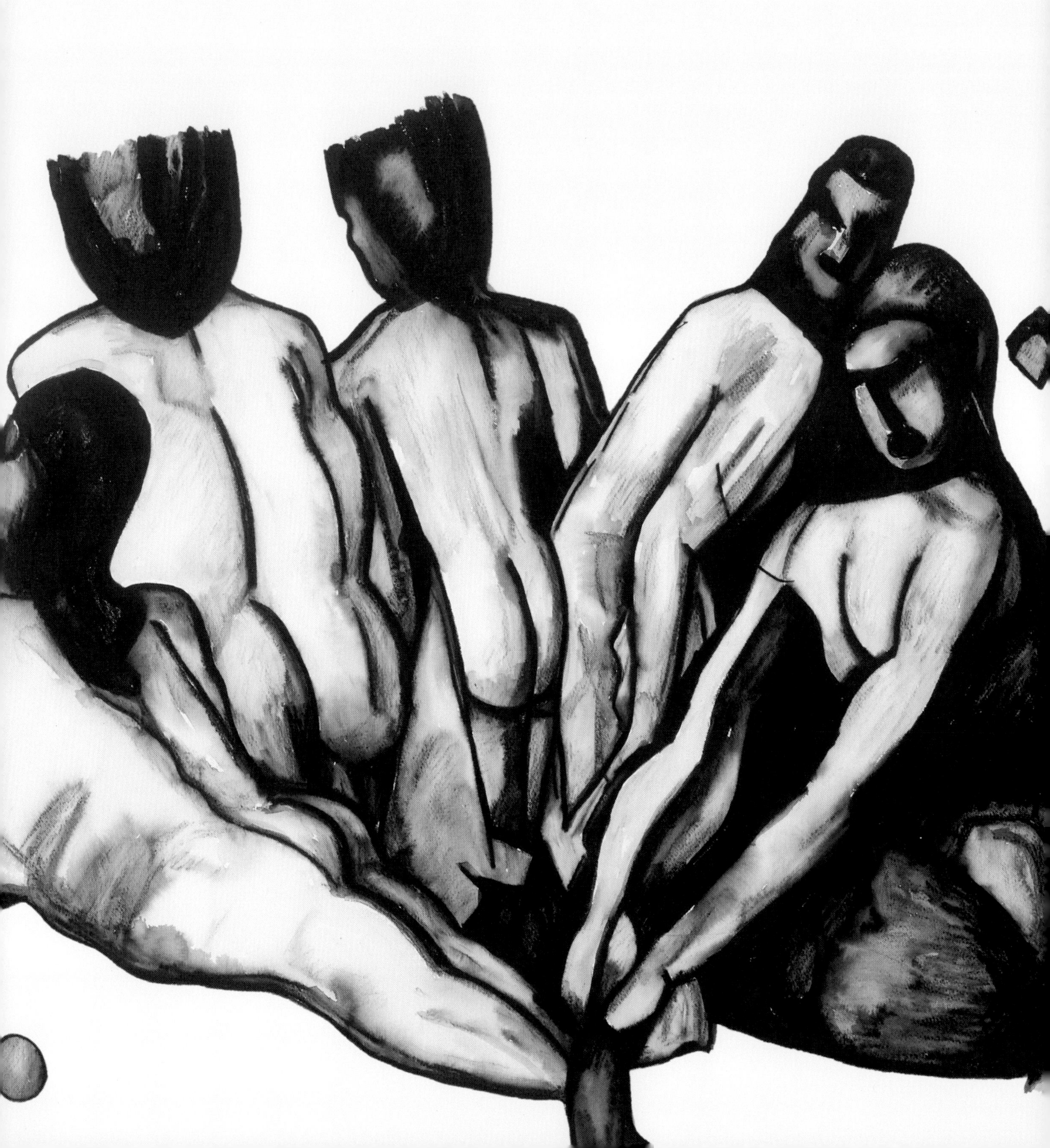

# Cézanne at the Whitworth

Richard Thomson

Karsten Schubert's bequest of works on paper by the great French artist
Paul Cézanne to the Whitworth Art Gallery is both outstandingly generous
and remarkably well directed. Cézanne (1839–1906) was one of the beacons
of modern art: a painter and draughtsman whose highly original work and
independent personality meant that it took time for his example to gain
traction, but who by the early twentieth century was being held up as a
guiding master – a position that has been unassailable ever since. A gift of
drawings or prints by him would be warmly received by any museum, but
a donation of such extent and variety is altogether remarkable.

The Karsten Schubert bequest includes drawings as well as prints – both
black-and-white and colour lithographs and etchings – of diverse subjects,
from portraits and bather scenes to landscapes and copies after past art.
As a group it strikingly enhances the Whitworth's world-famous collection
of works on paper, centred on its celebrated holdings of English watercolours,
notably its great group by J.M.W. Turner. But this gift of works by Cézanne
magnifies the importance of another major field: nineteenth-century French
drawing. The national collections in the United Kingdom are fortunate to
have some remarkable holdings of French works on paper from that period,
as are the Ashmolean Museum at Oxford and the Fitzwilliam Museum at
Cambridge. As is typical, these have generally been gradually accumulated
by purchase and gift, but there have been some notable contributions in the
form of bequests from single collectors. César Mange de Hauke's bequest of
16 works on paper to the British Museum in 1968 represented a wide range
of examples, from a portrait drawing by Jean-Auguste-Dominique Ingres to
a monotype made in Tahiti by Paul Gauguin. Perhaps the outstanding works
of the De Hauke bequest are the two *essence* drawings by Edgar Degas and
the pair of studies for Georges Seurat's *A Sunday on the Grande-Jatte* (1884–86,
Art Institute of Chicago): one of the empty landscape and the other of the
dominant couple. Another highly noteworthy bequest in this area was that
of Andrew Gow to the Fitzwilliam Museum in 1978. This gift of some 60
drawings, as well as a number of paintings and bronzes, spans from Eugène
Delacroix to Henri Matisse, but 15 drawings by Degas form its core. These
range from copies he made of Italian painting and sculpture as a student in
the 1850s to a charcoal of a nude dancer made about 1900. Such concentrated
gifts deepen a wider collection immeasurably, and it is in their distinguished
company that Karsten Schubert's bequest belongs.

Schubert's gift of Cézanne works on paper similarly augments an already
impressive collection; indeed, it may be the jewel in its crown. Arriving
as a lecturer in history of art at the University of Manchester in 1977, with
responsibility for teaching nineteenth-century French art, I was curious to

find out what the university's art collection had to offer, and on investigation was both surprised and delighted. There were over 80 sheets, covering a wide gamut of graphic media over a long chronological range. While the Whitworth had no works by Ingres or Delacroix, this was compensated by a highly finished watercolour by Paul Delaroche related to *The Execution of Lady Jane Grey* (1833, London, National Gallery) and an exquisite study in coloured chalks for his *Childhood of Pico della Mirandola* (1842, Musée d'Arts de Nantes). Appropriately enough, given the major significance of the Whitworth's collection of English watercolours, there were also notable landscape drawings by French artists, from painters of the Romantic era such as Adrien Dauzats and Alexandre-Gabriel Decamps, to Eugène Boudin, Henri Harpignies and Auguste Lepère, to luminous early twentieth-century works by the Neo-Impressionists Paul Signac and Henri-Edmond Cross. Nor were artists of great renown missing from the Whitworth's collection. There was a dynamic drawing by Henri Daumier, related to his heart-rending group of travelling players, and two drawings of peasants by his friend Jean-François Millet. The artists who exhibited at the Impressionist exhibitions of the 1870s and 1880s were represented by two works by Degas – one an outstanding large pastel of a seated young woman and the other a fascinating counter-proof of a ballet subject from the late 1890s – as well as a pastel of an industrial river scene by Armand Guillaumin (fig.2) and no fewer than four drawings in various media and of different subjects by Camille Pissarro. The collection also included a watercolour by Cézanne of a clearing in a wood, dating probably from the 1890s. The great surprise to me was two large drawings from different phases of Vincent van Gogh's short career: one a highly finished watercolour and gouache of the fortifications of Paris, made in 1887, and the other a brush drawing of harvested fields dating from the last weeks of his life, in 1890. With the encouragement of the Whitworth's keeper, the late Francis W. Hawcroft, and Michael Clarke, then assistant keeper of prints (and later director of the National Gallery of Scotland), I catalogued the collection for an exhibition, *French 19th Century Drawings in the Whitworth Art Gallery*, staged from 2 May to 28 June 1981. It should be recorded here that I misattributed a splendid watercolour, *View of Rouen* (fig.3), to Théodore Rousseau when it is by Paul Huet, and failed to credit to Paul Gauguin a remarkable mixed-media drawing of 1889 (*In Brittany*, fig.1), despite the insistence of my wife Belinda. Nevertheless, the exhibition and catalogue established the Whitworth collection's considerable importance in this field.

With the Karsten Schubert bequest, that importance has been much magnified. Cézanne's work on paper is now represented in its full range, the Whitworth's landscape watercolour *Study of Trees* (*La Lisière*) (cat.16), acquired

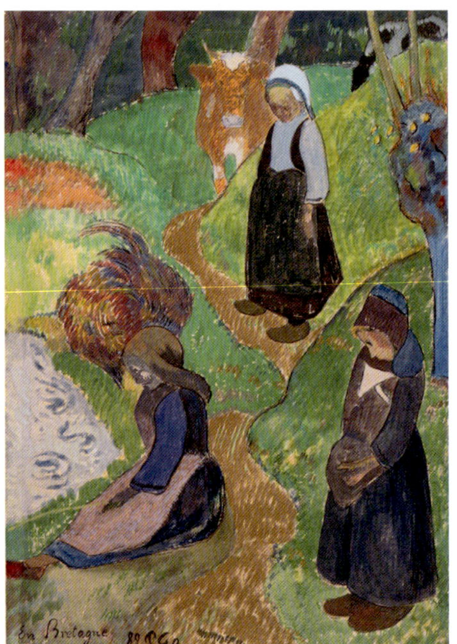

Fig.1
Paul Gauguin, *In Brittany* (*En Bretagne*), 1889
Watercolour and gouache on paper, 37.7 × 27 cm
The Whitworth, The University of Manchester,
D.1926.20
Purchased from the Leicester Galleries, London,
1926

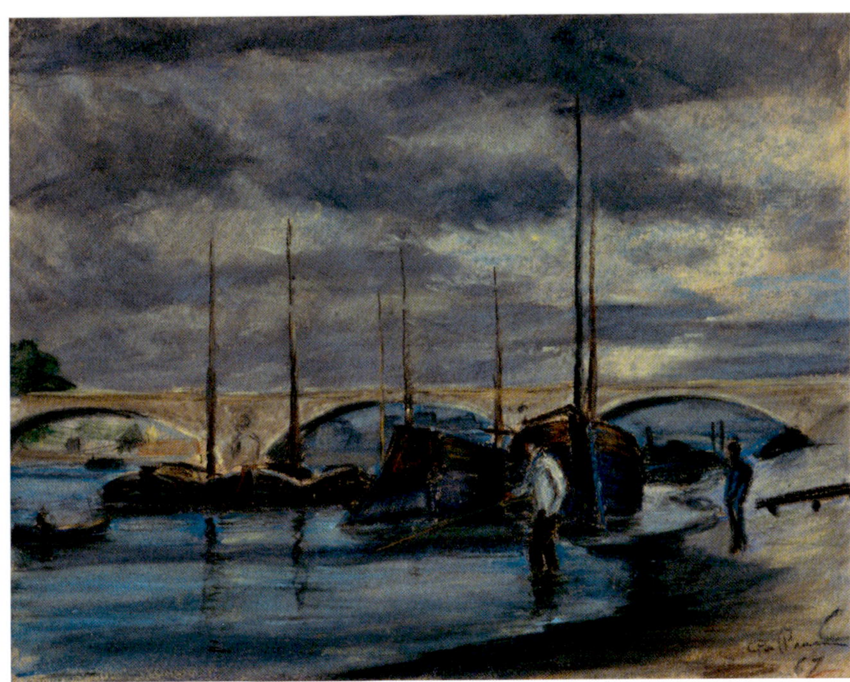

Fig.2
Armand Guillaumin, *Le Quai de Bercy*, 1867
Pastel on paper, 23.8 × 28.2 cm
The Whitworth, The University of Manchester, D.1951.4
Gift of Margaret Pilkington, 1951

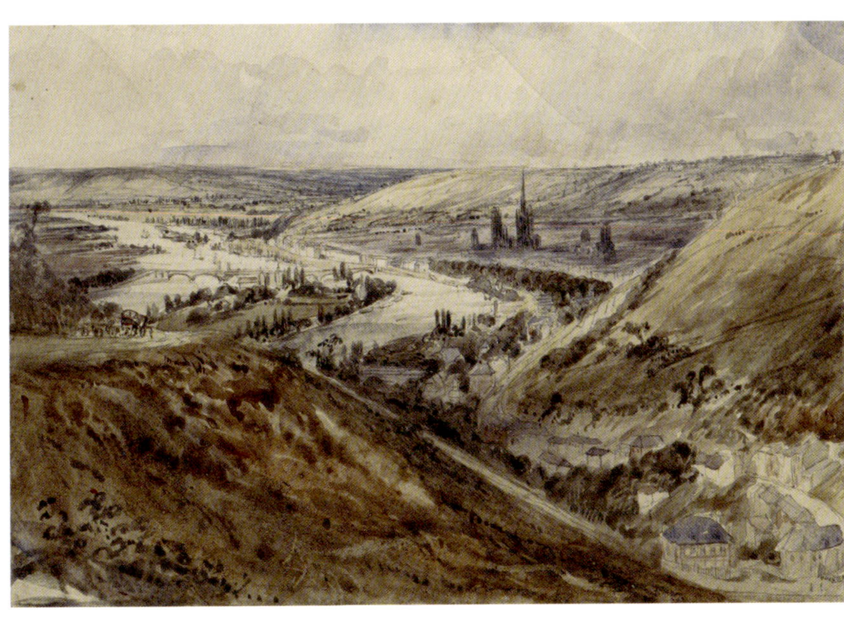

Fig.3
Paul Huet, *View of Rouen*, 1831
Watercolour and pencil on paper,
19.5 × 29.2 cm
The Whitworth, The University of
Manchester, D.1925.31
Purchased from Messrs Cremetti, 1925

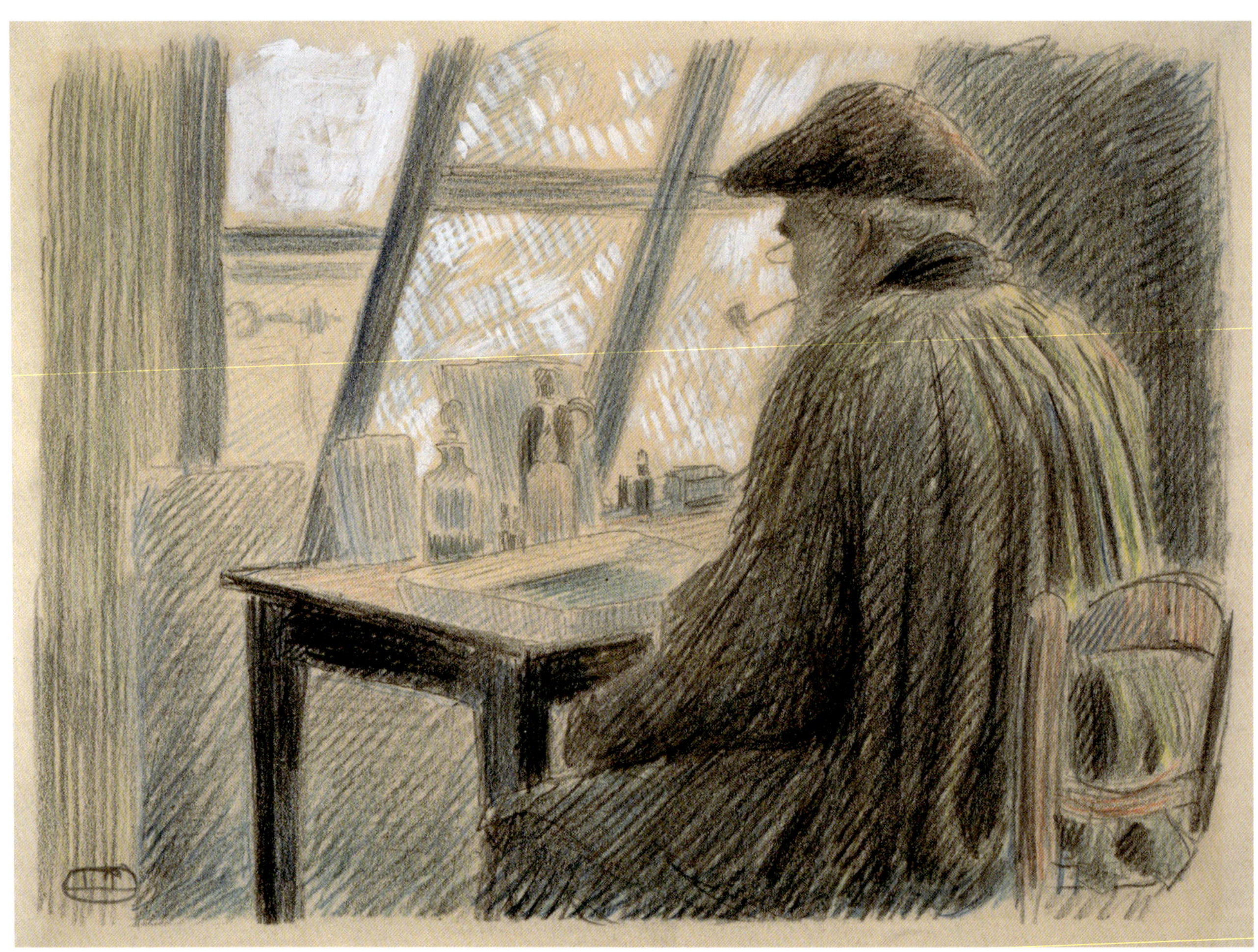

Fig.4
Lucien Pissarro, *Camille Pissarro Etching*, c.1896
Pencil and chalk on paper, 14.6 × 20.3 cm
The Whitworth, The University of Manchester,
D.1946.9
Presented by Esther Pissarro in memory of her
husband, 1946

in 1927, now supplemented by work in pencil of various kinds – from rapid notations of ideas and observations to more attentively observed pieces – as well as examples of the prints, both etchings and lithographs, with which Cézanne sporadically occupied himself. The range of the Whitworth's Cézanne holdings becomes clear if one runs through the works more or less chronologically, considering clusters and themes. The earliest drawing, dating from the later 1860s, is a dramatic scene in which three men, arriving from the left, impel themselves towards a reclining woman and her companion, who seem to shrink from them (cat.3). The subject is unknown; it might be historical or biblical, or perhaps a scene from a seventeenth- or eighteenth-century French drama. This small but intense theatrical subject needs further research; it is thus ideal for a university art gallery's collection.

In 1872 Cézanne spent time with the older painter Camille Pissarro (fig.4) at Pontoise, north of Paris, and in 1873 was introduced to Dr. Paul Gachet, who lived at nearby Auvers-sur-Oise. These two encouraged Cézanne to make etchings. *Head of a Young Woman* (cat.4), a small but direct and intense print, was made in September 1873. *Landscape at Auvers* (cat.6), also made that year, is highly simplified, with economical treatment of the buildings and trees. Its intense inking is reminiscent of Gachet's own etchings and its compact motif recalls Cézanne's painting *La Maison du pendu* (*The House of the Hanged Man*, 1873; Paris, Musée d'Orsay), shown at the first Impressionist exhibition the following year. Another 1873 etching represents the painter Armand Guillaumin (cat.7), like Pissarro a fellow exhibitor with the Impressionists; a marginal sketch at top left, of a man hanging from the gallows, associates this informal portrait with the group's work in Auvers that year. An etching by Pissarro of Cézanne (cat.8), made the same year as their first controversial exhibition, reinforces the collective identity of this loose group. Cézanne's thick jacket and overcoat, practical cap and untrimmed beard depict him as a farouche man of the outdoors but do not specify him as an artist. However, by intriguing contrast, in a lithographic self-portrait made more than 20 years later (cat.17) Cézanne introduced the right-angled edge of a stretched canvas or drawing block to indicate his creative identity, for otherwise the bourgeois costume of waistcoat and bow tie and the rather timid, even troubled, gaze would scarcely present him as an artist.

One fascinating drawing has three quite different subjects, for Cézanne could be inclined to use the same sheet for unrelated motifs (cat.12). The largest element is an affectionate head of his son, also called Paul, born in 1872. His chubby face suggests an age of about ten, and Cézanne modelled his features in the simplified planes that he had begun to develop in the later 1870s. Alongside the portrait are two other drawings, one of a female bather

seen from behind, moving to her right – a figure that recurs, with slight
variations, in several compositions with which Cézanne began to preoccupy
himself from this period – and the other of the draped head of Ceres, copied
from a composition by Peter Paul Rubens that Cézanne probably knew via a
reproduction. The nude figure was Cézanne's choice in two other drawings
from the bequest. One is after the *Venus of Vienne* (cat.15), a crouching marble
figure from the first or second century BC of a kind typical in Graeco-Roman
art. Excavated in the Rhône valley some 50 years earlier, it was purchased by
the Musée du Louvre in 1878 and Cézanne copied it soon afterwards, relishing
the rhythms of breast and folded flesh when seen from the side. Another
sheet is a copy after the dramatic *Milo of Croton* (1671–82) by the Marseille
sculptor and architect Pierre Puget (cat.11). Cézanne, himself from Aix, greatly
admired his fellow Provençal, making over 50 copies of his work and even
painting the house where Puget had been born (*Houses in Provence: The Riaux
Valley near L'Estaque*, c.1883; Washington DC, National Gallery of Art). At the
Louvre Cézanne often copied the *Milo of Croton*, which was originally made
for the gardens at Versailles. The pathos and torment of Ovid's story of the
old warrior attacked by a lion upon getting his hand trapped in a tree trunk,
rendering him helpless, attracted Cézanne, whose copy caught the sculpture's
agonised torsion.

Cézanne's fascination with the bather subject recurs in the important
drawing *Five Bathers* (cat.9), squared for transfer and linked to a major
painting of 1885/87 now in the Kunstmuseum Basel (fig.5 and p.56). The
grouping of this composition suggests narrative and interchange. There are
five naked women at a pool, one of them seated in the water at the centre.
She looks up from her vulnerable position to the figure leaning in from the
left, who seems to raise one hand in a gesture of admonition. Virginia Spate
has suggested that this evokes the myth of Diana and Callisto. Diana was the
virgin huntress, and Cézanne seems to have represented the moment when
one of her attendant maidens – on the left – stripped off Callisto's drapery
to reveal her pregnancy, the goddess – the figure at far right – imperiously
gesturing her expulsion to be turned into a bear. Cézanne's love of classical
literature makes plausible such a reading. For their part, Cézanne's male
bather subjects do not seem to cohere into such narratives. His young men
are shown in general and likely poses of stretching, resting and bathing in
sylvan settings. This is exactly what Cézanne had done as a teenager with
Aixois school friends such as Émile Zola. His images of male bathers are
recollections of their shared youth and are also loosely associative with the
classical education they received and the lingering notion of a Mediterranean
Arcadia that it prompted. During the mid-1890s Cézanne made two

Fig.5
Detail of Paul Cézanne, *Five Bathers*, 1885/87
Oil on canvas, 65.3 × 65.3 cm
Kunstmuseum Basel, G 1960.1

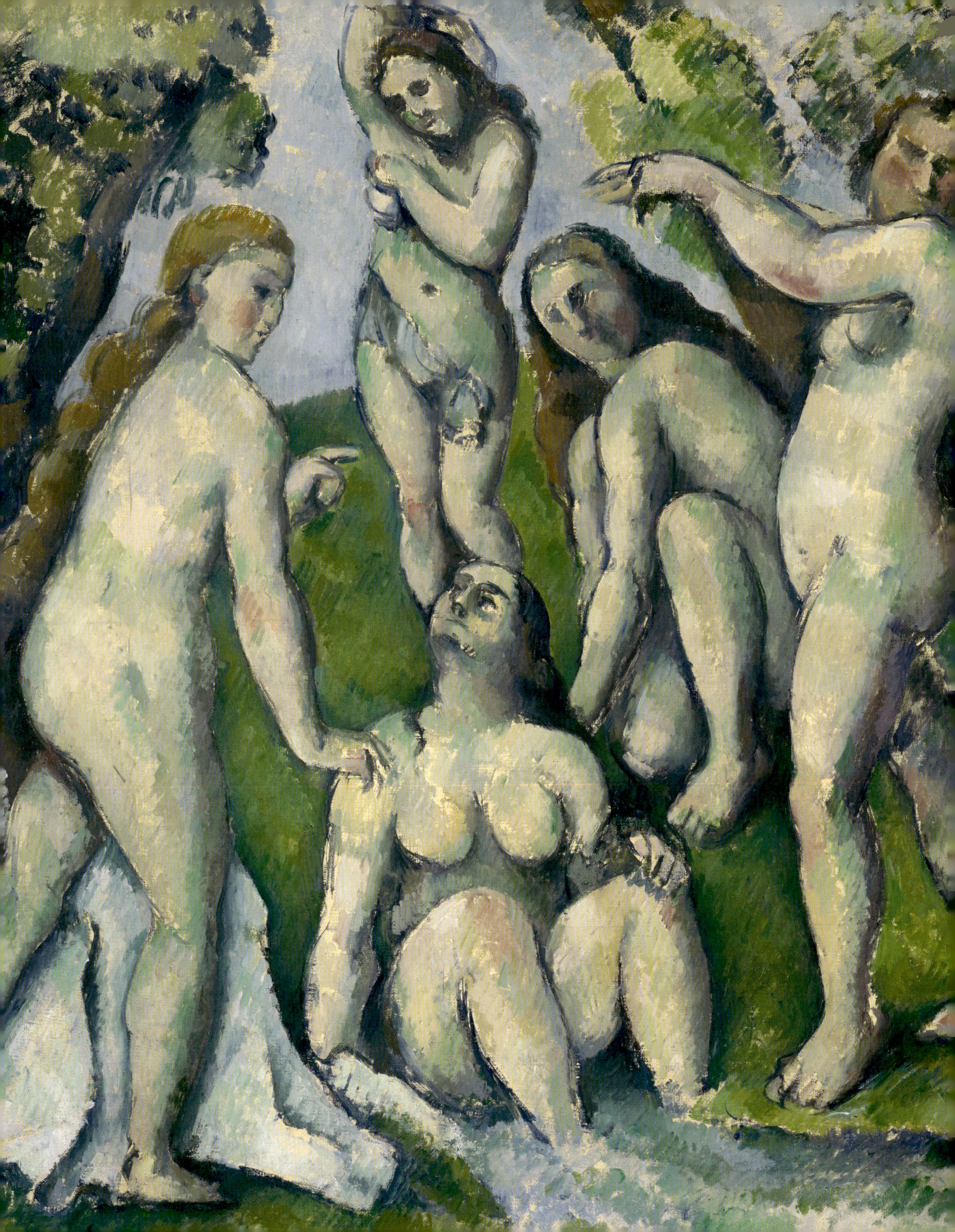

lithographs of such compositions, the most important of which is a colour print (cat.19) based on the composition of a painting exhibited at the third Impressionist exhibition in 1877, *Bathers at Rest* (p.74, c.1876–77; Philadelphia, Barnes Foundation). Whereas the central figure is apparently wearing modern trunks, the pose of his companion on the right is based on the antique sculpture of *Cincinnatus*, which Cézanne knew from the Louvre and copied. Thus this *Bathers* composition is a fusion of the contemporary and the classical in Cézanne's native setting, the Montagne Sainte-Victoire, the great mountain ridge to the east of Aix, seen in the landscape's background.

Finally, the bequest includes a strongly modelled drawing of a human skull (cat.14). Skulls featured in a number of Cézanne's still lifes across a variety of media. In his later years, especially after his diagnosis of diabetes, the image may have acted as a *memento mori*, but in earlier work the skull may have been linked to Cézanne's awareness of the work of another former school friend, Antoine-Fortuné Marion, who in 1880 became director of the Muséum d'Histoire Naturelle in Marseille and who had discovered Neolithic remains, including skulls, in caves on Montagne Sainte-Victoire. The motif therefore had local, as well as personal, associations.

With the addition of such a splendid group of Cézanne's works on paper the Whitworth's already impressive collection of nineteenth-century French drawings is mightily strengthened. With the existing collection, interesting comparisons could be made – between the work of Jean-François Millet and Pissarro, for instance, or Henri Fantin-Latour and Georges Seurat. The Schubert gift will enhance such conjunctions, Cézanne's etching of Guillaumin being contemporaneous with the Whitworth's pastel by the latter, for example, or Cézanne's bathers with a similar subject by Ker-Xavier Roussel (fig.6), who visited him in Aix in 1905. Karsten Schubert's generous bequest immediately makes the Whitworth one of Britain's outstanding collections of works by Cézanne. With such a gift the value lies not just in the objects themselves but in the ongoing role they will play in the collection as a whole, bringing into play interrelationships and continuities that will resonate in the scholarly community. As a group of great works of past art that will form the basis for future research, this outstanding bequest is an ideal enhance-ment for a university collection such as the Whitworth.

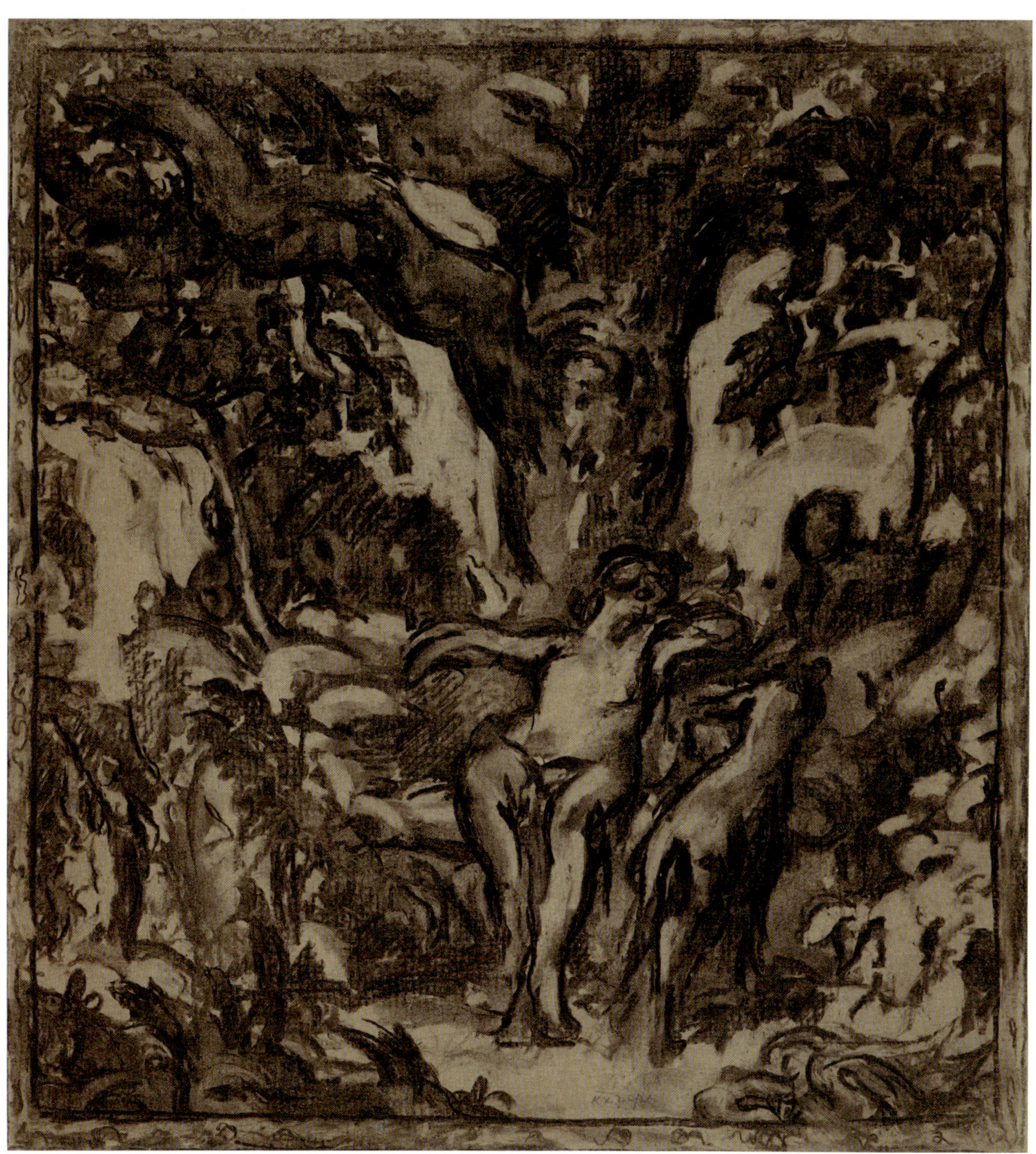

Fig.6
Ker-Xavier Roussel, *Pastorale*, c.1925
Oil on paper laid on panel, 45.1 × 41.9 cm
The Whitworth, The University of Manchester,
D.1945.5
Presented by Sir Thomas D. Barlow, 1945

# On Looking at Cézanne

Christopher Lloyd

Paul Cézanne (cat.8) is one of those relatively few European artists whose works have a resonance that has extended well beyond their lifetime. This applies equally across the paintings, drawings and prints that comprise his extensive oeuvre. The authoritative nature of his paintings is more easily appreciated, for they hang on the walls of museums and galleries, whereas his drawings and prints, for sound conservation reasons such as avoiding overexposure to light, are less accessible and accordingly less well known. Yet there can be no doubt that Cézanne's drawings in particular have proved to be highly influential in the development of modern art, to the extent that every mark he made on paper is worthy of close scrutiny and careful interpretation. This can only be truly said of a very few other artists, and those are of the very highest calibre: Leonardo da Vinci, Michelangelo, Dürer, Rembrandt and Rubens.

Recognition of Cézanne's genius during his lifetime was slow and controversial, not simply because of his stylistic and technical innovations but also because of his proud independent spirit, aspects of his quixotic personality and his commitment to the Mediterranean culture of southern France. Born in Aix-en-Provence in 1839 into a relatively well-off family, Cézanne was educated and received his first training as an artist locally. These formative years coincided with the founding of the Félibrige Society, promoting a 'Provençal Renaissance' via interest in its regional language, customs and festivals. Notably, at a later stage in his life Cézanne adopted one of the dominant historical landmarks in Provence, namely the Montagne Sainte-Victoire, as his personal symbol, which for him had almost spiritual connotations. Consequently, it features prominently in many of his landscapes (cats 19 and 20).

The majority of Cézanne's early friendships were with the writers, scientists and artists associated with the 'Provençal Renaissance', including the novelist Émile Zola, with whom he shared a love of classical literature and texts by French authors. The subject matter of some of Cézanne's first compositions was inspired by written sources, as well as by the desire to emulate themes made popular by earlier masters and the wish to pursue his own, often erotic and scatological, interests (cat.3). Indeed, it was said that his love of literature was so ardent that, if he had not chosen to become a painter, he could well have been a poet.

Realistically, however, success as an artist in late nineteenth-century France could only be achieved or sustained in Paris, which was then the centre of the art world. The city provided facilities for training and outlets for exhibitions, as well as the possibility of attracting the attention of critics and dealers and the support of intrepid collectors. For most, the Salon, sponsored by the state, was where aspiring artists sought public recognition, but by the 1860s, in spite of some initial teaching reforms, the supremacy of the Salon was being challenged by avant-garde movements initiated by the Impressionists and Post-Impressionists. Cézanne reached Paris in 1861, at a time of great artistic change and one pregnant with new possibilities. He began by trying to follow the normal path to winning official acceptance, but, failing to gain admittance to the prestigious École des Beaux-Arts, he instead attended the more open-minded Académie Suisse, where he met Camille Pissarro, Claude Monet and Armand Guillaumin (cat.7). Here, for a nominal fee and surrounded by kindred spirits, Cézanne was able to develop his own style as a result of the Académie Suisse's more relaxed approach to copying, more informal attitude to drawing from the posed model and less purist stance on the choice of materials.

Challenging the hegemony of the academic system, avant-garde artists cultivated more spontaneous methods and techniques. There was now an emphasis on working out of doors directly in front of a motif, with freer brushstrokes and purer colours; above all, the whole process of creating a work of art – from the method of preparation to the application of paint and degree of finish – was governed by a less formal process. These new stylistic proclivities revealed a different set of priorities and skills, ones that were more appropriate to the depiction and recording of aspects of everyday life – subjects far removed from the historical, religious and mythological scenes encouraged at the École des Beaux-Arts and preferred by the Salon. Cézanne participated in two of the eight Impressionist exhibitions held between 1874 and 1886: the first, in 1874, and the third, in 1877. Yet even when his work was seen in the company of his *confrères*, it was regarded by critics and public alike as virtually incomprehensible.

From the start, Cézanne's art was uncompromising. His manner of painting and drawing could be overwhelmingly powerful and rugged, almost aggressively so. In his earliest works this style matched the violence of the scenes he chose to depict. This moment is often described politely as being Cézanne's 'romantic' period, but he himself referred to it as his *manière couillarde* – roughly translated, his ballsy style. It was Pissarro who tamed Cézanne by helping him to control his emotions when confronting nature and by encouraging him to analyse motifs with greater care, to construct his compositions with more deliberation and to exercise stricter control over his brushwork. The two artists worked together during the 1870s and early 1880s, often side by side and on many occasions depicting the same landscape. No doubt on such occasions they discussed ideas relating to the anarchist philosophy that they both espoused, which upheld artistic freedom and the

autonomy of the individual. By the mid-1880s and the 1890s, when Cézanne
was spending an increasing amount of time in Provence, he had become
– rather belatedly, perhaps – a mature artist with a highly distinctive style
whose pictures, while not yet appreciated by the public, were beginning to be
favoured by pioneering collectors (cat.10) and a younger generation of artists.
Indeed, it is not simply from statements made in his letters that we know so
much about Cézanne and his ideas about art, but also thanks to the recollections of those followers who visited the increasingly reclusive artist in his
studio at Les Lauves, on the outskirts of Aix-en-Provence – artists and writers
such as Émile Bernard, Joachim Gasquet, Maurice Denis, Jules Borély and
Léo Larguier. In effect, Cézanne became a legend in his own lifetime (cat.17).

A compulsive worker, Cézanne was tormented by self-doubt throughout his life. Even just two years before he died in 1906, aged 67, he wrote:
'I am proceeding very slowly. Nature appears to me very complex, and the
improvements to be made are never-ending'.[1] The search that begins in his
drawings is not brought to a close in the traditional sense in his paintings,
since in both he was relentlessly investigating the best way to realise in
visual terms the sensations that he was experiencing before nature, and,
what is more, to do this as accurately and truthfully as possible. For Cézanne,
drawing and painting were to all intents and purposes subject to the same
preconditions, and he pursued them with the same end in mind. This is self-
evidently the case with the late watercolours, dating from the 1880s onwards,
where the medium is often handled in an almost exploratory way. In both
his paintings and drawings Cézanne sought the definitive, but it was a search
that could result in uncertainty or lead to a cul-de-sac. Yet, as the critic David
Sylvester expressed it, the search often amounted to a form of 'uncertainty
made beautiful'.[2]

Cézanne's known works on paper number roughly 1,500 drawings and
600 or so watercolours. By contrast, his output of prints is negligible and
surprisingly conservative in approach, as though the medium did not inspire
him as it did Degas, Pissarro and Mary Cassatt. The bulk of the drawings were
originally made in sketchbooks of varying sizes. Only seven of these have
survived intact with their linen covers, but others (at least 18) are identifiable
and can be partially reconstructed. Several more may have been destroyed, and
perhaps yet others remain to be discovered. It seems that Cézanne used these
sketchbooks randomly, often ignoring page sequences and never working on
just one and filling it up fully. This diffuseness and disregard for sequencing
makes individual sheets from the sketchbooks notoriously difficult to date.
Some drawings, especially those with watercolour or the more finished
examples, were extracted by the artist's heirs, often for sale; many of the

sketchbooks were broken up in this way and single sheets dispersed far and wide, making their reconstruction a complicated and often protracted exercise that is still in progress today.

An overall examination of the works on paper reveals various preferences. Many drawings are in pencil of varying hardness, sometimes heightened with touches of watercolour (cat.16). Pen and ink occurs only occasionally at the start of Cézanne's career, and softer media (black chalk and charcoal) feature intermittently, with pastel appearing only once. Watercolour is often associated with the second part of Cézanne's career and regularly on sheets intended to be independent works of art in their own right, for sale (marks from the pins used to keep the paper in place while being worked on are frequently visible in the corners). However, there are several early watercolour or mixed-media works by Cézanne, and several Provençal artists in the first half of the nineteenth century, such as François Marius Granet, had been fine exponents of watercolour.

The success that Cézanne gained in the last decade of his life, mainly through promotion by the dealer Ambroise Vollard (1866–1939) and then by the Galerie Bernheim-Jeune, was in part due to the outstanding technical quality of his watercolours, with their carefully applied patches of colour, luminous but subtly calibrated tones blending with the white of the paper, and, most difficult of all, the evocation of atmosphere however mundane or grand the subject, whether an interior or exterior. Some of the watercolours appear to be unfinished, but in fact they have been brought to the degree of finish that Cézanne perceived as sufficient for recording the world as he saw it with the greatest possible verisimilitude (cat.16). In these respects Cézanne is comparable with J.M.W. Turner.

The essence of Cézanne as an artist lies just as much in the works on paper as in the paintings, particularly since there is an almost perfect overlap in subject matter. There is considerable diversity in the choice of motifs, but the scope is limited insofar as each idea is explored with an intensity that is almost myopic: landscapes, still lifes, portraits, copies of Old Masters and certain compositional ideas, such as the male and female bathers, which he repeated frequently, not in series but as sets of variations. On pages in the sketchbooks the artist's mind can be seen moving from informal studies of his wife and child (cats 12 and 13), for example, to the further development of compositions that were in the forefront of his mind, or even preliminary thoughts for a new one as yet unexplored (cat.14).

Radical though he may have been seen by his contemporaries, Cézanne honoured tradition. Like Degas, he made numerous copies after works by older masters – paintings (cat.11) and sculpture (cats 11 and 15) – as well as after works by those contemporaries or immediate predecessors whom he respected (particularly Eugène Delacroix). He registered as a copyist at the Musée du Louvre in 1863 and 1868 and worked at the Musée de Sculpture Comparée in the Palais du Trocadéro (opened in 1882). He also cut out illustrations of works of art from journals and magazines, collected reproductions of works of art and often consulted published sources on the history of art. These he kept with him for reference, and many are recorded among his possessions in his last studio at Les Lauves. Copying was axiomatic to the training process for young artists, but Cézanne carried it to far greater lengths as a way of solving problems pertinent to his own work and as a way of honing his skills. As he reflected at the very end of his life, 'In my opinion, one does not replace the past, one only adds a new link'.[3]

A perfect example of the dichotomy in Cézanne's work between tradition and innovation is found in his predilection for scenes of male and female bathers. He had indeed witnessed such scenes for himself on the banks of the river Arc to the south of Aix-en-Provence, but at the same time he was reflecting on the Arcadian images made by Renaissance painters such as Giorgione and Titian, or works by seventeenth-century artists such as Rubens, Poussin and Domenichino. These earlier painters were in turn evoking a classical ideal still promulgated, for example, at the École des Beaux-Arts. But Cézanne was concerned with a newer, more modern version of the Garden of Eden. He clearly hoped to reinvigorate a readily identified subject central to mainstream European art through fresh configurations and groupings that achieved a greater resonance with contemporary life while at the same time validating the new art that he was pioneering (cats 9 and 18–21).

Cézanne was an intensely private man, and drawing is essentially a private preoccupation. He was not a precise or accurate draughtsman in the academic sense. Sometimes his drawings can seem inept, clumsy or outright failures, but to dismiss them as such is to misunderstand their purpose. They are in reality tokens of a lifelong struggle with himself and the artistic ideals that he upheld. They were a way of keeping a sense of failure at bay while incorporating the determination never to give up and to carry on to the very end. It was this palpable tension, harnessed to his iron determination and single-mindedness, that Picasso admired as the '*inquiet*' of Cézanne's art.

All drawings made by Cézanne, extending from the slightest scrawl to the most dedicated compositional study squared for enlargement (cat.9), are part of a process based on unusual powers of visual analysis and sensitivity in execution. Added to this combination is a remarkable level of technical accomplishment, complemented by an intellectual probity that has rarely, if ever, been surpassed in European art.

1  Paul Cézanne, letter to Émile Bernard, 2 May 1904, in John Rewald (ed), *Paul Cezanne's Letters*, Bruno Cassirer, Oxford, 1976, p.302.
2  David Sylvester, *Looking at Giacometti*, Chatto & Windus, London, 1994.
3  Paul Cézanne, letter to Roger Marx, 23 January 1905, in Rewald, *op. cit.*, p.313.

# Catalogue

1

# Marcantonio Raimondi (after Raphael)

*The Judgment of Paris*, c.1513–18

Engraving, 29.2 × 43.3 cm
Bartsch 245
The Whitworth, The University of Manchester, P.3081
Presented by George Thomas Clough, 1921

Few images have had a greater impact on the history of Western art than Marcantonio Raimondi's *Judgment of Paris*. Characterised by intense shadows, brilliant areas of light and subtle gradations of tone, this masterful engraving derives from a lost design that Raphael created based on the study of two damaged ancient sarcophagi in Rome.

The engraving shows the dramatic dénouement of a fateful beauty pageant by the shores of the river Ida at a banquet in celebration of the marriage of Peleus and Thetis. Eris, goddess of discord, who was not invited, arrived intent on creating havoc. She threw a golden apple from the Garden of the Hesperides into the festivities as a prize for the fairest, setting off a competition between Juno, Venus and Minerva, who all claimed the title. They turned to Jupiter – hovering in the clouds at upper right with lightning bolt in hand – to settle the dispute. But he demurred, passing the task to the Trojan mortal Paris, who had earlier demonstrated fairness in judging a dispute concerning two bulls, still visible in the upper-left corner of the print.

Paris sits on rumpled drapery as the three goddesses undress before him, guided by Mercury, who is identified by his winged cap and caduceus. With an attentive dog and peacock by his side and shepherd's crook in his left hand, Paris carefully passes the apple to Venus, who had promised him Helen of Troy in return. A winged genius crowns Venus with laurels, while her son Cupid playfully rustles the fabric draped around her. Apollo, racing through the heavens in his chariot encircled by the zodiac, peers down at this fateful moment of choice, which would launch the Trojan War and ultimately lead to the founding of Rome.

The nude bodies stand out in dramatic relief. They appear sculptural and monumental despite the small size of this intricate engraving. Marcantonio may have used a pumice to roughen the surface of the printing plate, creating the subtle patches of grey that distinguish the Whitworth's outstanding impression of this quintessential Renaissance print. Generations of artists have turned to this image for inspiration. Édouard Manet famously and scandalously recast the suggestive grouping of two reclining river gods and a nymph at far right as a modern-day picnic scene in his *Le Déjeuner sur l'herbe* (1863, Paris, Musée d'Orsay), originally exhibited under the title *Le Bain*.

EW

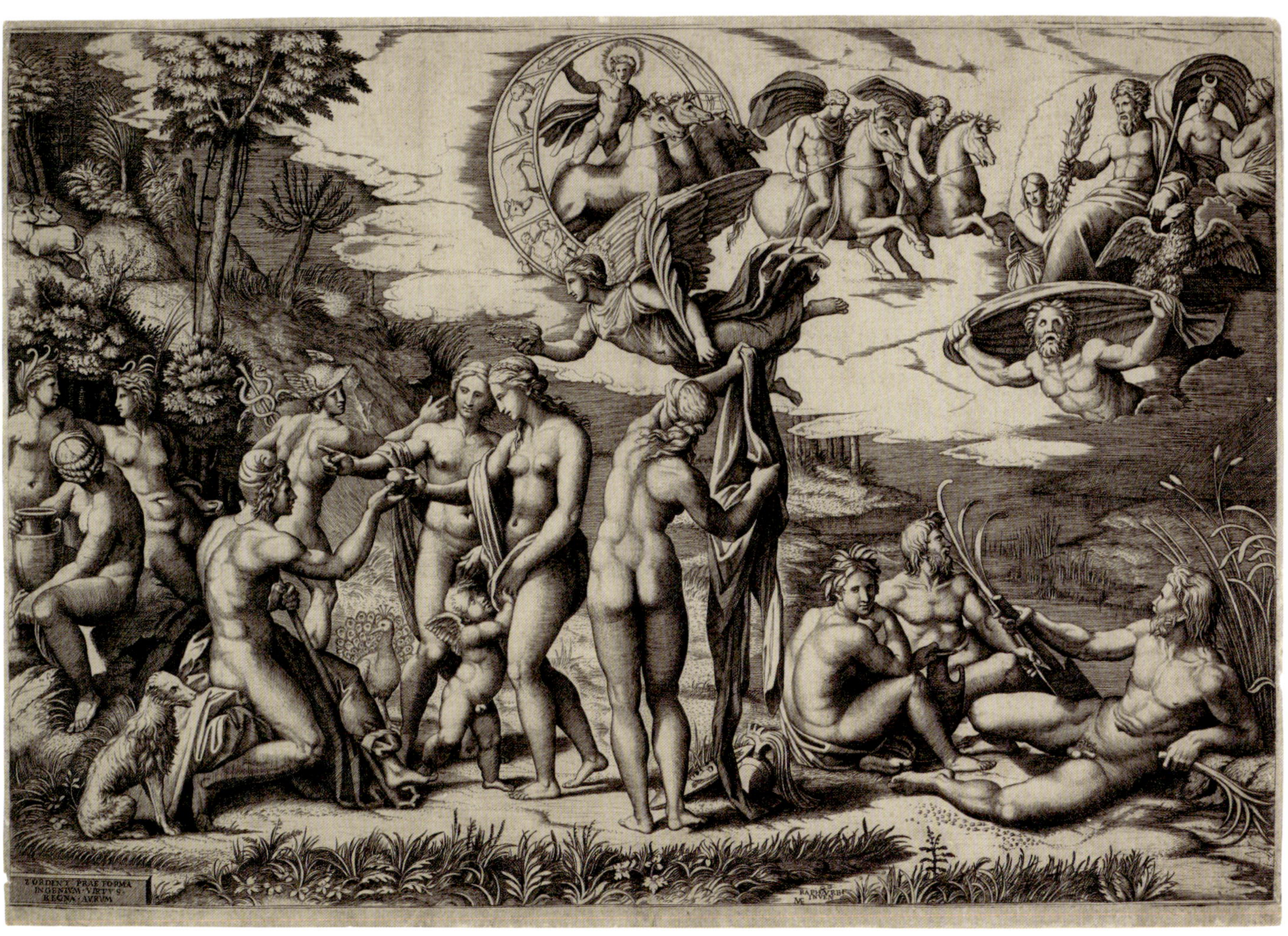

SORDENT · PRAE · FORMA
INGENIVM · VIRTVS
REGNA · AVRVM
RAPH · VRBI · INVEN
MF

2

Anonymous engraver after Marcantonio Raimondi
*Venus, Cupid and Minerva*, c.1530

Engraving, 17.7 × 11.5 cm
Bartsch 310
The Whitworth, The University of Manchester, P.20417.2
Bequeathed by William Sharp Ogden, 1926

Marcantonio Raimondi's *Judgment of Paris* gave rise to a vast number of interpretations in many artistic media, including paintings, majolica, bronze and tapestries, as well as other prints. The small, worn engraving before us extracts three figures from the centre of Marcantonio's *Judgment of Paris*: Venus with her child Cupid at left, and, at right, Minerva. Isolated from the composition and provided with only minimal setting, these nudes seem out of place. They are no longer actors in an important mythology but appear instead to be frozen in time and space as strange studies in the treatment of the classical nude from multiple angles.

The great early nineteenth-century print cataloguer Adam von Bartsch classified this engraving as an anonymous print by a 'fairly mediocre' talent – possibly a pupil of Marcantonio, but certainly not the master himself.[1] For all its shortcomings, the print testifies to the enormous popularity of Marcantonio's work, which was not limited to the appeal of his erudite subjects, refined technique or even his masterful approach to composition and narrative, but also extended to his treatment of the body. The Whitworth's impression is badly damaged, particularly in the upper-right corner. Pristine impressions that have not been trimmed measure 23.2 by 13.4 centimetres and include a large blank expanse above the figures.[2] Although we do not know the function of the small engraving, the marred condition of this impression suggests that it may have attracted the attention of artists who studied these decontextualised figures for their archetypal beauty. It clearly also appealed to collectors eager for any image, however modest, of Marcantonio Raimondi's exemplary translation of Raphael's graceful bodies into print.

EW

1 Adam von Bartsch, *Le Peintre-graveur*, 21 vols., Degen, Vienna, 1803–15, vol.14, p.234, no.310.
2 Rainer Michael Mason and Mauro Natale, *Raphaël et la seconde main: Raphaël dans la gravure du XVIe siècle, simulacres et proliferation*, Musée d'Art et d'Histoire, Geneva, 1985, p.520, no.62.

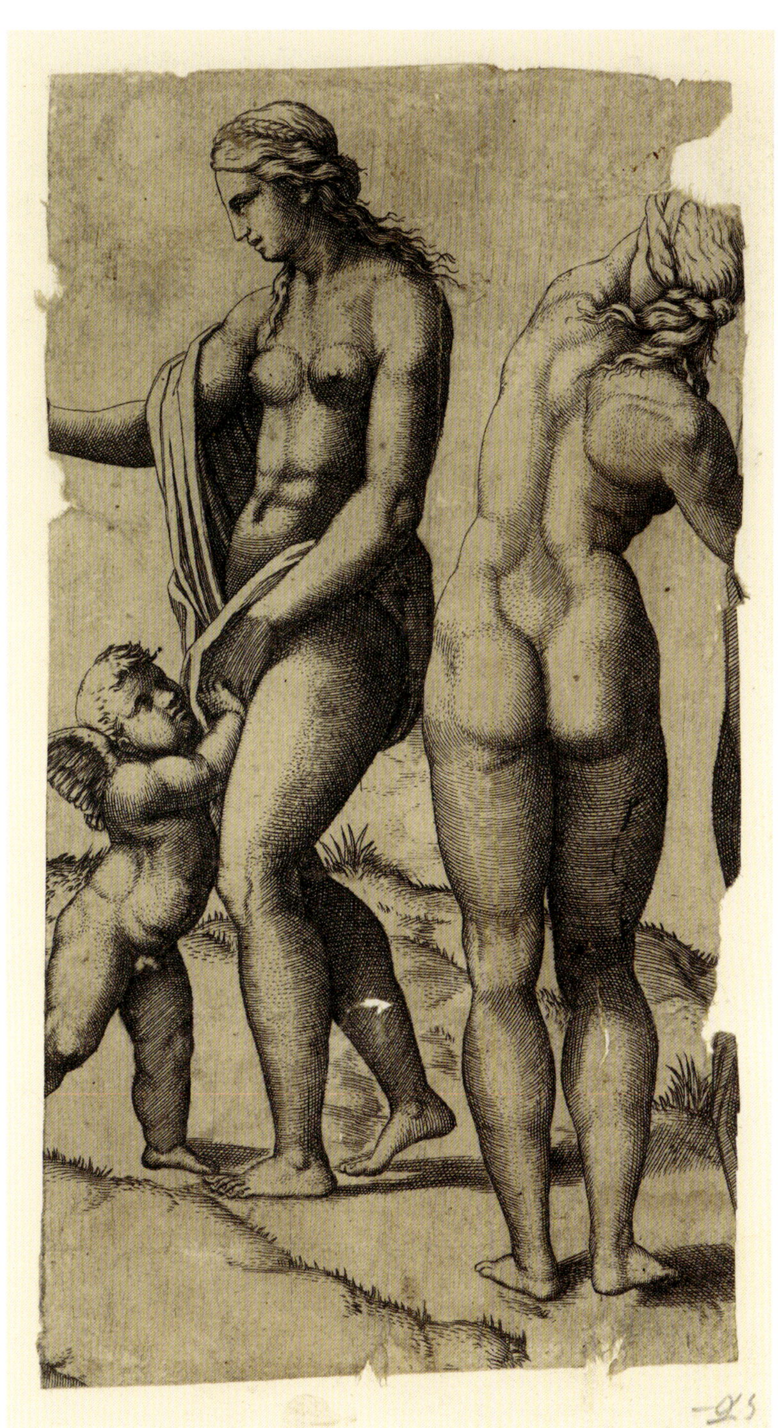

3
Paul Cézanne
*A Historical or Biblical Scene: The Rape of Lucretia (?)*,
1865–69

Pencil on paper, 11.7 × 17.2 cm
Chappuis 125A; Feilchenfeldt/Warman/Nash 1811
Estate of Karsten Schubert, on extended loan to The Whitworth,
The University of Manchester

In this crowded composition, a woman turns frantically between the figures that surround her. The man in the foreground has his hand on her thigh, its grip on her flesh emphasised with insistent shading. She reaches, or is pulled, towards a hastily sketched figure at right. The dark eyes and heavy patches of shading across the sketch are in keeping with Cézanne's thick and tenebrous painting style of the 1860s, which he later called '*couillarde*' (ballsy).

Scenes of sexual fantasy and violence are common in Cézanne's work of this period, summoned from his own imagination or borrowed from the history paintings and biblical scenes in the Musée du Louvre. This drawing has previously been euphemistically titled 'A Woman Caught Unawares', recalling the biblical story of Susanna, who is usually depicted with the lecherous voyeurs who falsely accused her. However, the turned wooden bedpost at centre and roughly sketched drapery of a curtain above the woman's head suggest a domestic setting.

This could be a historical subject taken from one of the classical texts that Cézanne read as a schoolboy in Aix-en-Provence. Livy's *History of Rome* tells the story of the Roman noblewoman Lucretia, who lived in the sixth century BC. Prince Sextus Tarquinius raped Lucretia, who then killed herself to spare her family from the perceived dishonour. The story of Lucretia and Tarquinius has been the subject of many artistic interpretations, but it is unusual for depictions to include so many figures; the two heads at top left could be unrelated.

This sheet was once part of a larger page of studies. The section originally to its left, featuring a skull, is today in the Harvard Art Museums (FWN 2227). The location of the other part, which was below this drawing, is unknown. A photograph of the original sheet shows that it repeats this composition, but with the two superfluous heads turned to face the woman. Studies for the woman's pose, in ink rather than pencil, are also found on a drawing in the Staatliche Graphische Sammlung, Munich (FWN 2219). The drawing of a man in a toga on that sheet could support the Roman source of this scene.

RMcK

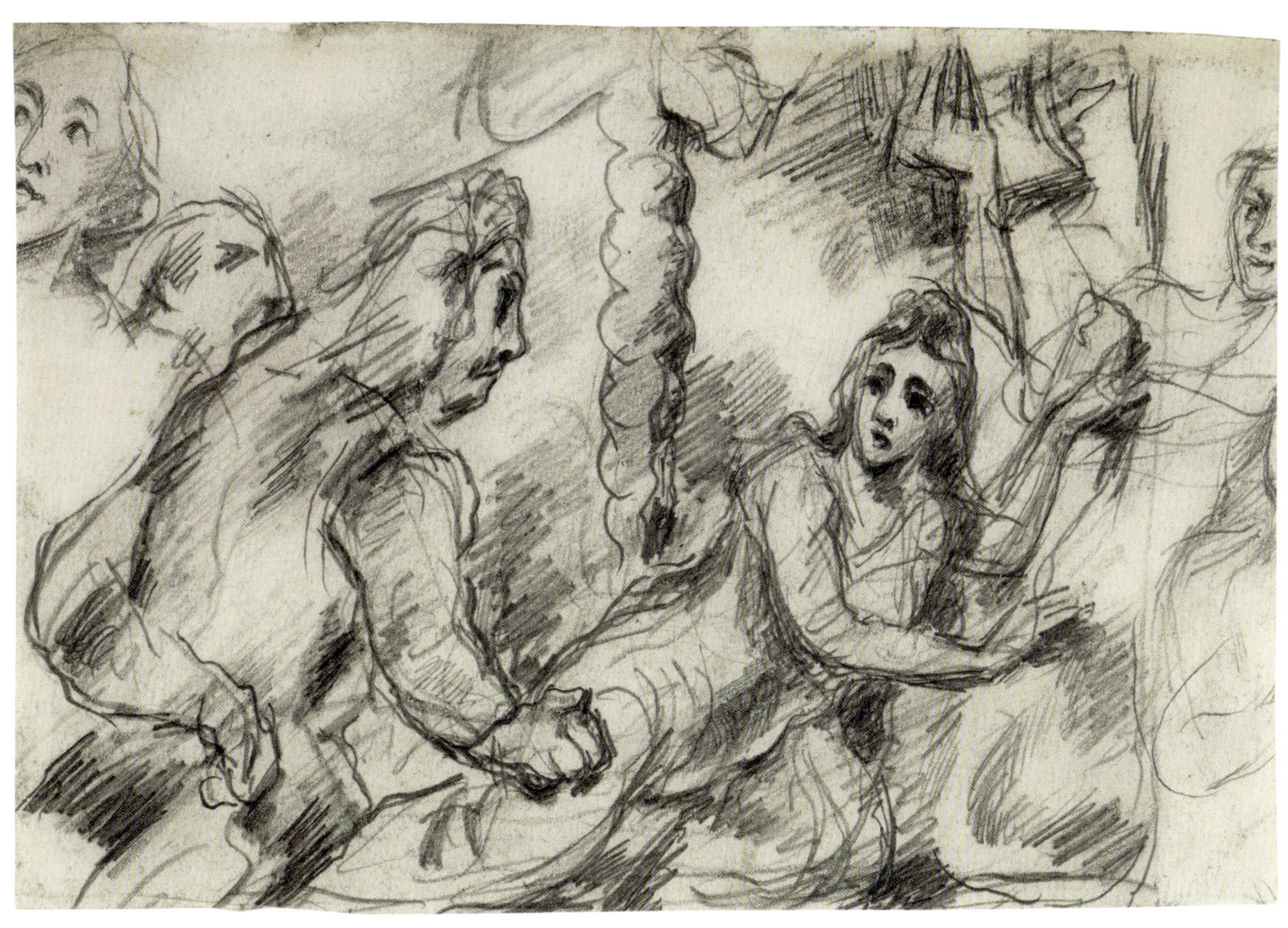

4
Paul Cézanne
*Head of a Young Woman*, 1873

Etching (second state of three), 12.5 × 10.2 cm (plate);
28 × 19 cm (sheet), Paul Gachet's own impression, as per his
inscription on reverse and collector's mark
Venturi 1160; Cherpin 4/ii (of iii)
The Whitworth, The University of Manchester, P.2019.4
Karsten Schubert, gift 2019

A young woman stares out impassively in this complex print.
She is Elmyre Roger, a neighbour of Dr. Paul Gachet (1928–1909),
a physician, amateur artist and friend of Cézanne. In 1873
Cézanne was living near Gachet in Auvers-sur-Oise, northwest
of Paris (see cat.6). Along with his friends Camille Pissarro and
Armand Guillaumin (see cats 7 and 8), Cézanne visited the
printmaking studio that the doctor had created in his granary.
As evident in the two impressions of this print (see also cat.5),
he was encouraged to experiment with the tools, plates, inks
and press therein.

Cézanne shows the young woman in *contre-jour*, with the
light emanating from behind and her face cast in shadow.
These extremes of light and shade offer the artist great opportunity to try out graphic techniques. Cézanne made three
states, reworking the copper plate for each, and impressions
in different inks, including the red-toned sanguine used for
this impression of the second state.

In the second state Cézanne introduced an instrument called
a roulette to tone the area to the left of the head. The roulette
wheel makes many tiny perforations, allowing the artist to
create an even area of shadow. The mechanical effect is in stark
contrast to Cézanne's agitated lines drawn freehand: with the
etching needle the artist incised diagonal lines across the outline
of the woman's face and body, his zigzags becoming loops at
bottom left. He created deeper shadows on her forehead, hair

and collar with vertical hatching. Bright highlights on her
right temple and the crown of her hair show that Cézanne had
carefully wiped ink from the plate.

For the third and final state of this print (cat.5), Cézanne
cut down the copper plate by a few millimetres on all sides.
This has the effect of making the composition more claustro-
phobic, as well as trimming the 'e' off the end of his signature
at bottom right. The larger paper size also makes the print
appear even more diminutive. The deeper shadow achieved
on areas of her face and dress, already hatched on the previous
state, may be the result of leaving more ink on the plate.

The distinctive collector's mark in the form of a cat on the
second state indicates that it originally belonged to Dr. Gachet.
He also signed the print on its reverse, beneath the inscription
'Tête de jeune fille Eauforte de Paul Cézanne – Auvers sur oise
– 1873 – Epreuve sanguine tirage ancien – 1873'. The doctor,
perhaps best known for having treated Vincent van Gogh,
owned numerous Cézanne paintings and works on paper.
Among them were two related 1873 drawings: a young woman,
possibly the same sitter, with her head cocked to the side and a
scarf covering her hair (Philadelphia Museum of Art; FWN 1710),
and Cézanne and Gachet preparing a copper plate, probably
for this very print, to be etched in acid (Paris, Musée d'Orsay).
RMcK

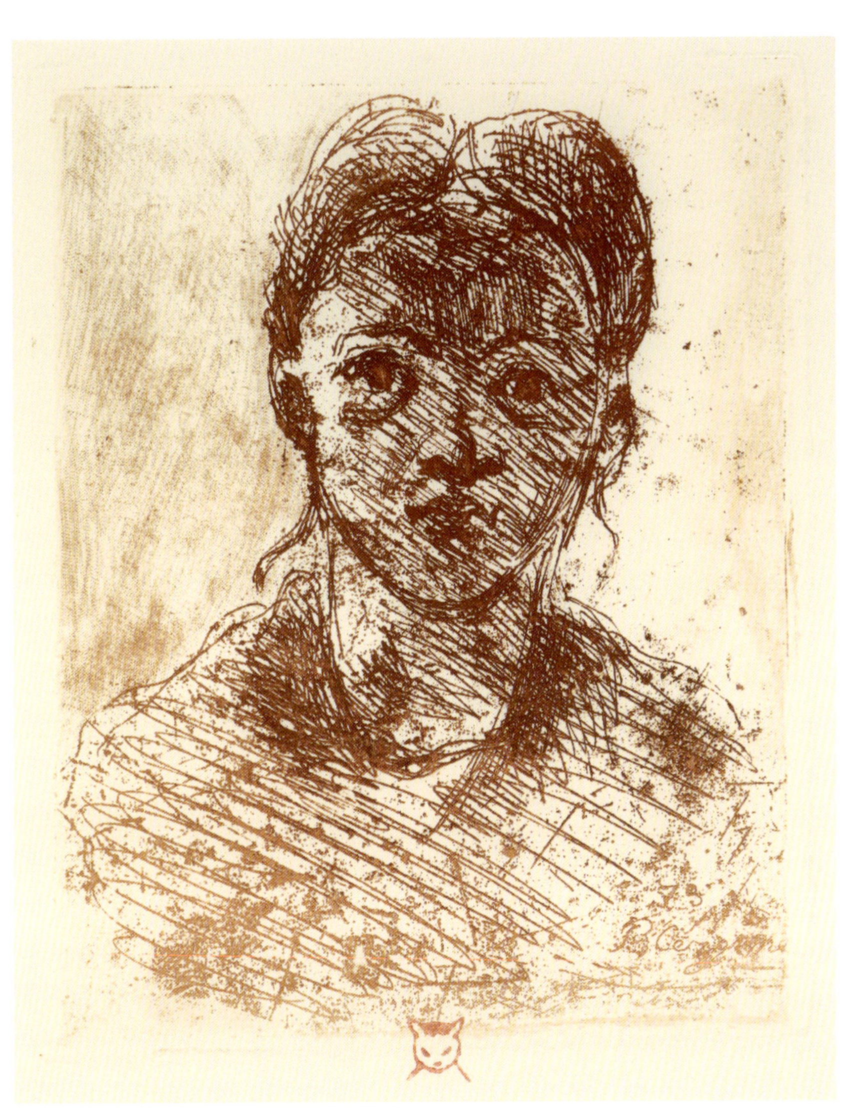

5
Paul Cézanne
*Head of a Young Woman*, 1873

Etching (third state of three), 12 × 9.5 cm (plate);
32.5 × 24.6 cm (sheet)
Cherpin 4/iii (of iii)
The Whitworth, The University of Manchester, P.2019.3
Karsten Schubert, gift 2019

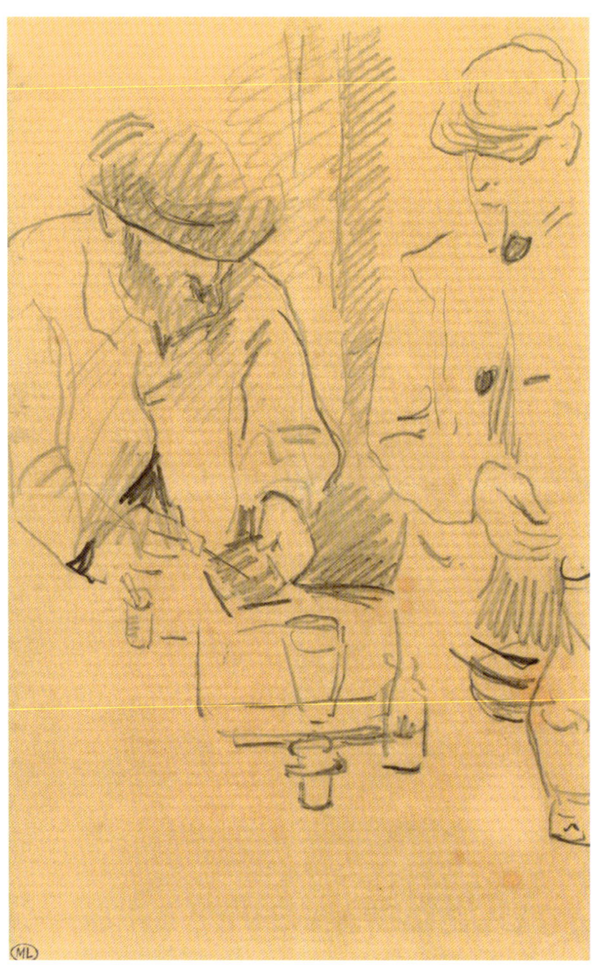

Paul Cézanne, *Cézanne Etching Next to Dr. Gachet, or The Bite*, 1873
Pencil on paper, 20.5 × 13 cm
Musée d'Orsay, Paris, RF 29925

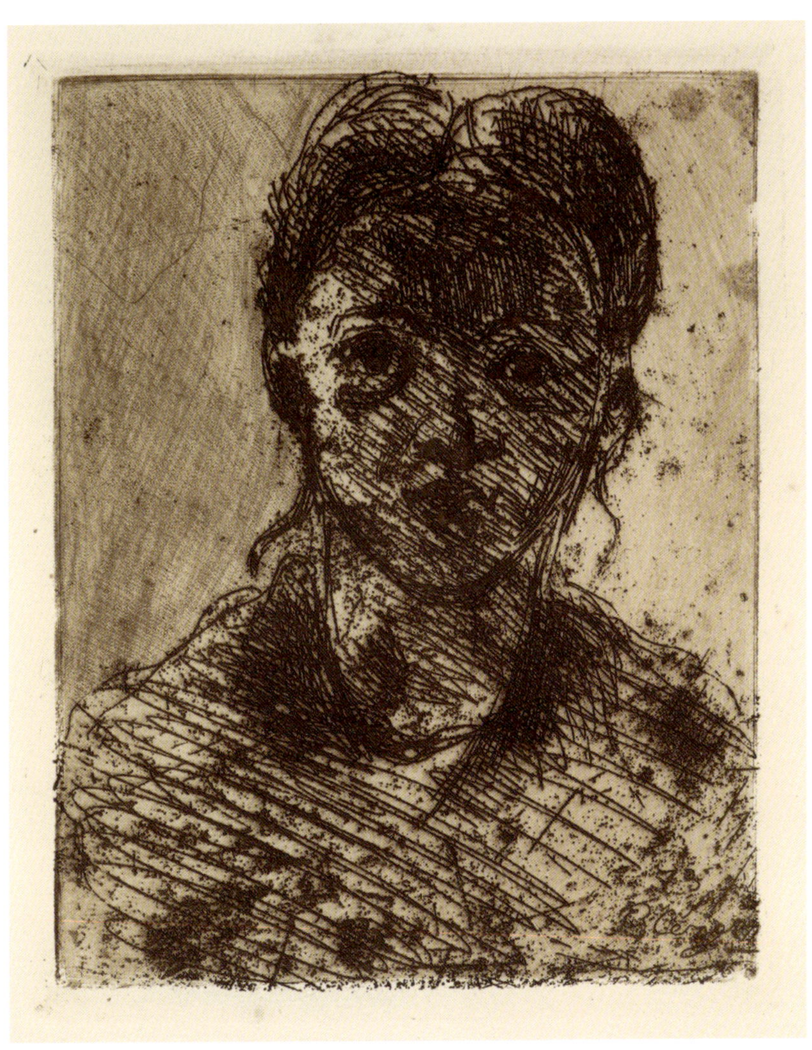

6
## Paul Cézanne
*Landscape at Auvers*, 1873

Etching, 13.5 × 9.5 cm (plate); 32.5 × 24.6 cm (sheet)
Venturi 1161; Cherpin 5
The Whitworth, The University of Manchester, P.2019.2
Karsten Schubert, gift 2019

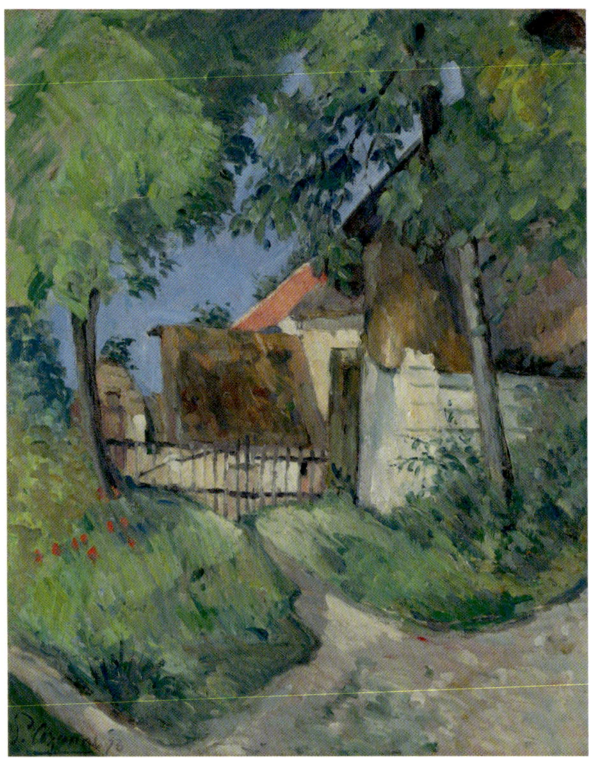

Paul Cézanne, *Entrance to the Farm, rue Rémy, Auvers-sur-Oise*, 1873
Oil on canvas, 60 × 49 cm
Private Collection (FWN 76)

In the summer of 1872, Cézanne, his partner Hortense Fiquet and their infant son, Paul, moved to Auvers-sur-Oise, which Cézanne depicts in this etching. The Parisian suburb on the river Oise had already attracted artists from the previous generation, including the great landscape painters Jean-Baptiste-Camille Corot and Charles-François Daubigny. Cézanne had his own artistic community around Auvers, where the young family lived until early 1874. His mentor Camille Pissarro (see cat.8) had moved to nearby Pontoise the previous year, and Armand Guillaumin (see cat.7) found work in the area. In this landscape and alongside these friends, Cézanne's painting style changed. He lightened his colour palette and shortened his brushstrokes. In the same period, a fourth friend in this group, Dr. Paul Gachet (see cats 4–5), encouraged Cézanne to take up printmaking.

This is the only example of Cézanne making an etching directly after one of his paintings, a landscape showing the nearby farm on rue Rémy, which he later gave to Pissarro (today in a private collection; FWN 76). This compact composition, with its rectilinear gate and buildings, suited translation into graphic form. Cézanne experiments with different kinds of mark-making, differentiating the forms of the buildings, rendered with neat, often parallel lines, from the fluid and lively delineation of the foliage around the path. He also goes to great pains to create the shadow at left, making repeated diagonal incisions. To balance this, he deviates from the painting's composition to leave the top right of the plate unmarked. Here the remaining ink on the plate picks up the grain of the paper.

This etching was used as the frontispiece for a book about Cézanne published in 1914, eight years after his death, by the Paris gallery Bernheim-Jeune, with texts by Octave Mirbeau, Théodore Duret, Léon Werth and Frantz Jourdain.

RMcK

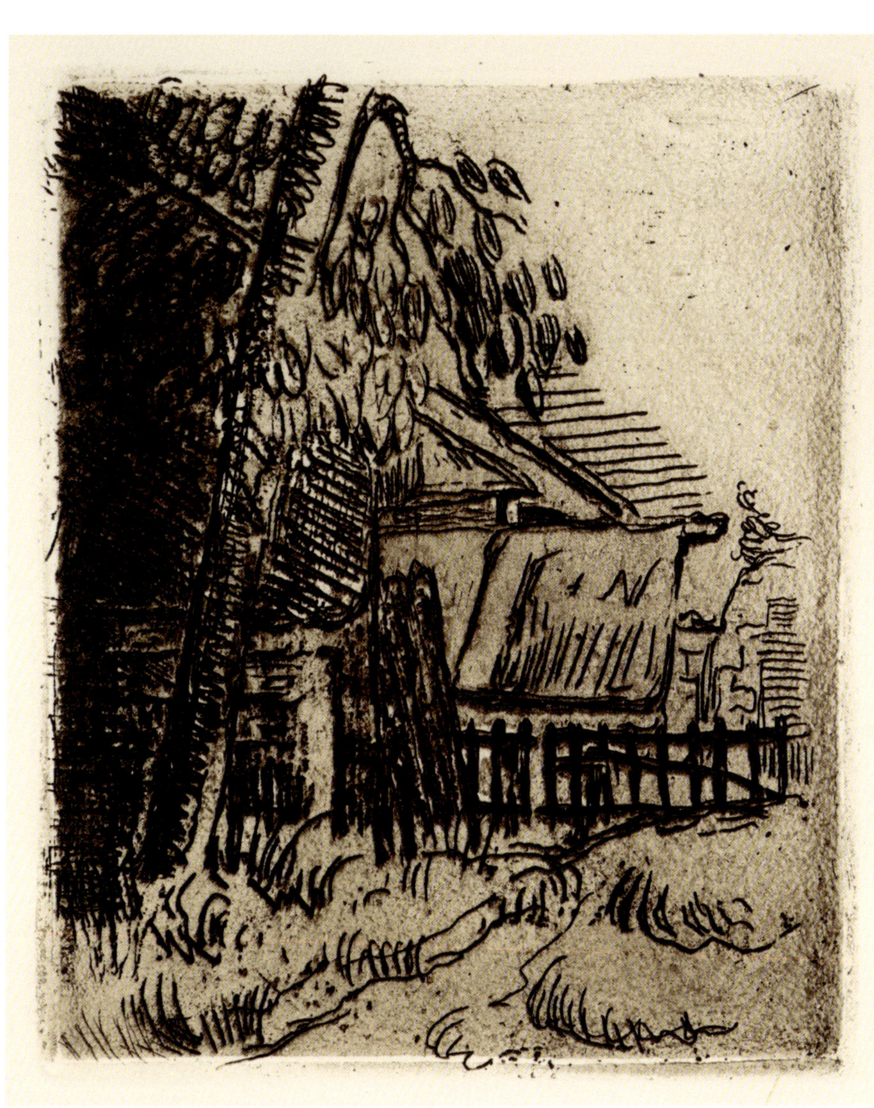

7
Paul Cézanne
*Armand Guillaumin with Hanged Man*, 1873

Etching, 14 × 10.75 cm (plate); 32.4 × 25.7 cm (sheet)
Venturi 1159; Cherpin 2
The Whitworth, The University of Manchester, P.2019.1
Karsten Schubert, gift 2019

Cézanne depicts his friend, fellow artist and sometime neigh-bour Armand Guillaumin (1841–1927) without formality or pretence. Sitting on the ground with arms folded and resting on his bended knee, the young man in hat and neckerchief looks out at the spectator directly. The portrait's simply drawn lines and the sporadic marks dotted across the image may reflect Cézanne's lack of experience in the medium and its homespun production, as much as the scene's casual nature.

Guillaumin and Cézanne met in 1862 during their training at the Académie Suisse in Paris. By necessity Guillaumin had to maintain his position as a civil servant, but he committed his spare time to his art. Over two decades the pair painted together periodically. Cézanne experimented stylistically by making copies after his friend's canvases. In the early 1870s, with their mutual friend Pissarro, Cézanne and Guillaumin frequented the printmaking studio of Dr. Gachet at Auvers-sur-Oise, where this etching was made. Cézanne's first print, *Barges on the Seine at Bercy*, was copied from a painting by Guillaumin.

The title of this print refers to the small rendering of a hanged man that appears in the top left. These few strokes of the etching needle are enigmatic. The perpendicular lines of the gallows might be read as the edge of a piece of paper pinned to the wall, suggesting this image is a drawing, print or playing card. The hanged man has been identified as Cézanne's visual signature, perhaps based on a nickname, but this is the only time it appears. The following year he painted a landscape in Auvers that he titled *The House of the Hanged Man* (Paris, Musée d'Orsay; FWN 81). Cézanne included that canvas in the first Impressionist exhibition in 1874, in which Guillaumin also participated. This portrait was used as an illustration in the *Histoire des peintres impressionnistes* published by Théodore Duret in 1906.   RMcK

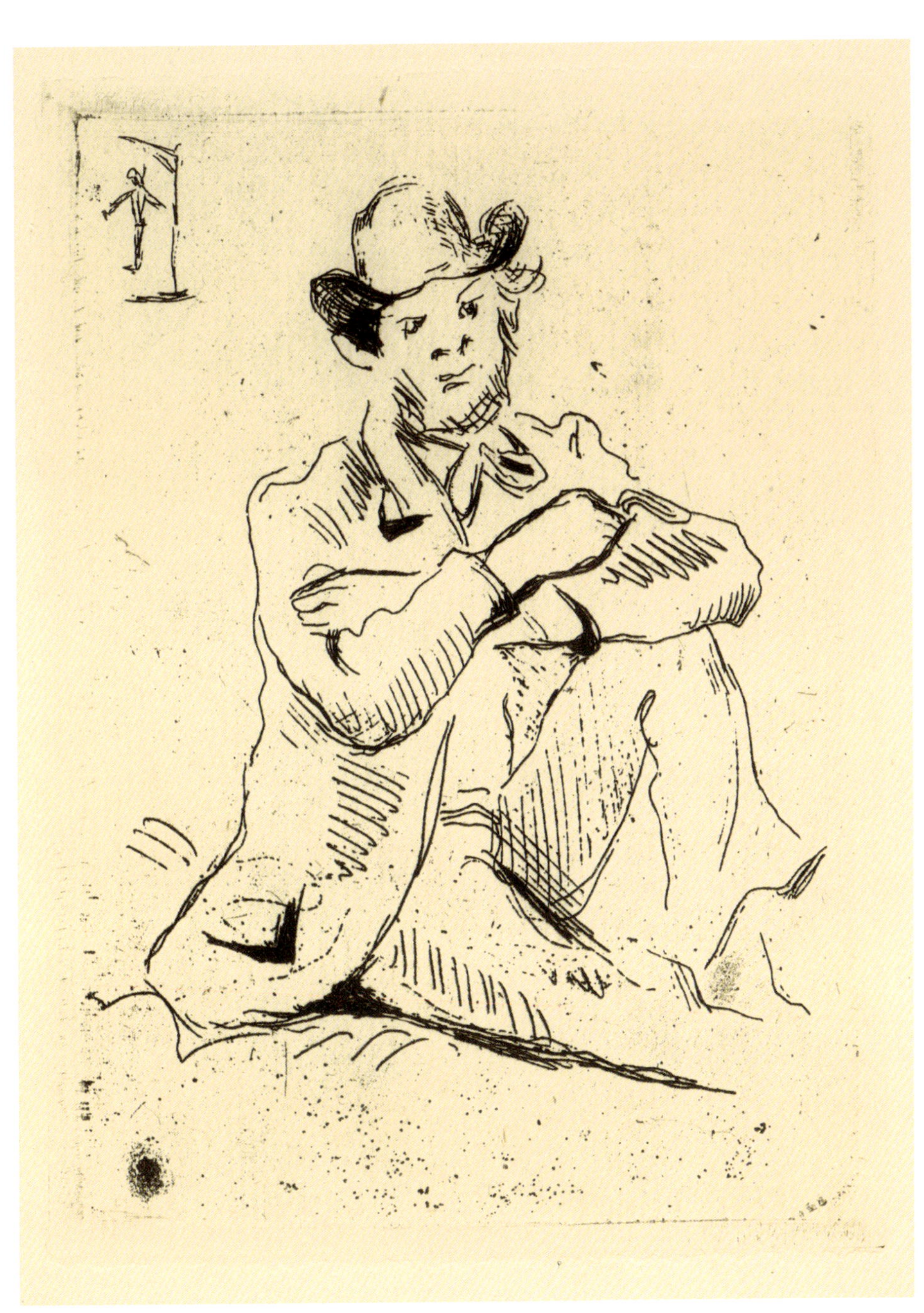

8

Camille Pissarro
*Paul Cézanne*, 1874

Drypoint, 44.8 × 29.2 cm
Gemeentemuseum, The Hague, 0016165

[Not included in exhibition]

Cézanne met the artist Camille Pissarro (1830–1903) in 1861, and they formed a friendship built on artistic kinship. Lasting over 20 years, it was one Cézanne's longest and most important relationships. In 1873–74, while living in adjacent Parisian suburbs along the river Oise, they painted the landscapes around their homes together and exhibited these works in 1874 at the first Impressionist exhibition (see cat.6). Pissarro, the older of the pair, had a considerable impact on Cézanne, evident especially in the lightening of his colour palette during this period. Pissarro was the more prolific printmaker, learning the technique a decade before Cézanne started to experiment with etching in 1873.

This is one of numerous drawn, painted or printed portraits Cézanne and Pissarro made of each other in this period. Pissarro succeeds in capturing Cézanne's forceful personality. Bold lines establish his features economically, including bushy beard and unruly hair protruding from a distinctive hat. The artist's imposing form is conveyed by the folds of the coat and cloak that fill much of the lower half of the print. His attire gives no indication of his profession, even if he is suitably dressed for painting outdoors. The previous year, Cézanne had drawn a full-length study of his friend kitted out for a session of painting *en plein air* (Paris, Musée d'Orsay).

This image reverses – by virtue of the print technique – Pissarro's 1874 painted portrait of Cézanne. The sitter wears the same outfit in each, bar the cloak. The painting's background is far more complex, alluding to Pissarro's esteem and aspirations for Cézanne: a painted landscape and prints of famous men are pinned to the wall behind the sitter.

In the early 1890s this print, partially coloured in flesh tones and shades of brown, was reproduced on the cover of an issue of *Les Hommes d'aujourd'hui* about Cézanne, the text written by Émile Bernard.

RMcK

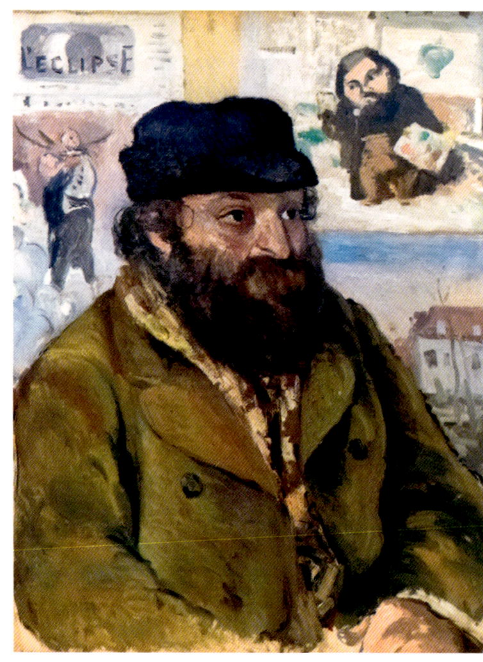

Camille Pissarro, *Portrait of Paul Cézanne*, 1874
Oil on canvas, 73 × 59.7 cm
On loan from the collection of Laurence Graff OBE
to the National Gallery, London

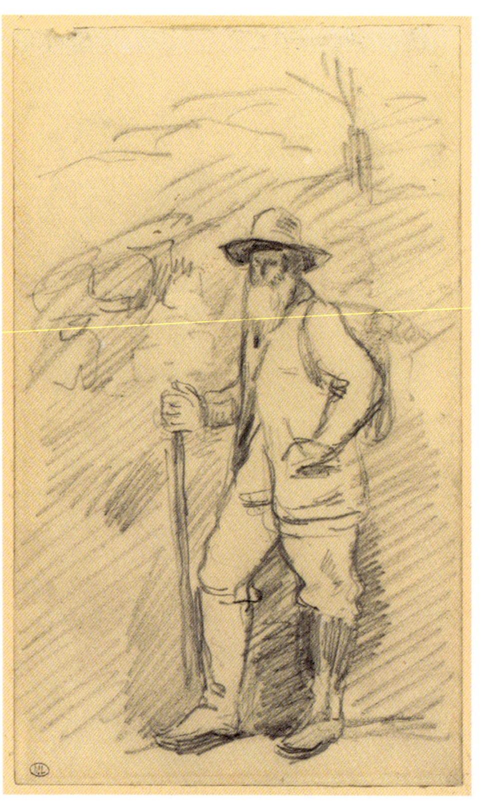

Paul Cézanne, *Camille Pissarro on his Way to the Motif*, 1873
Pencil on paper, 19.5 × 11.3 cm
Musée d'Orsay, Paris, RF 11995

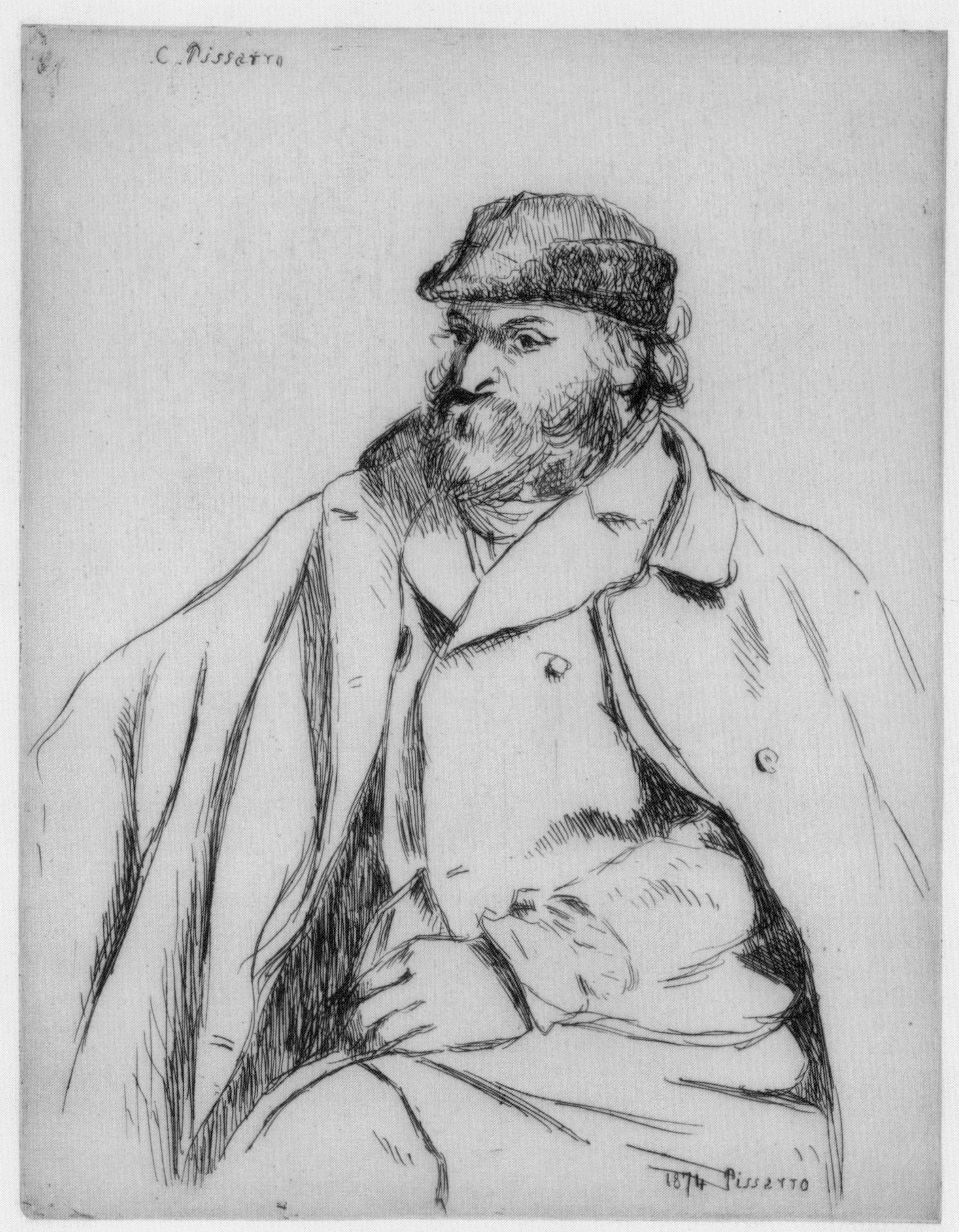

9
Paul Cézanne
*Five Bathers*, 1879–82

Pencil on paper, squared for transfer, 14.6 × 13.3 cm
Venturi 1490; Chappuis 517; Feilchenfeldt/Warman/Nash 2029
Karsten Schubert Ltd., on loan to The Whitworth,
The University of Manchester

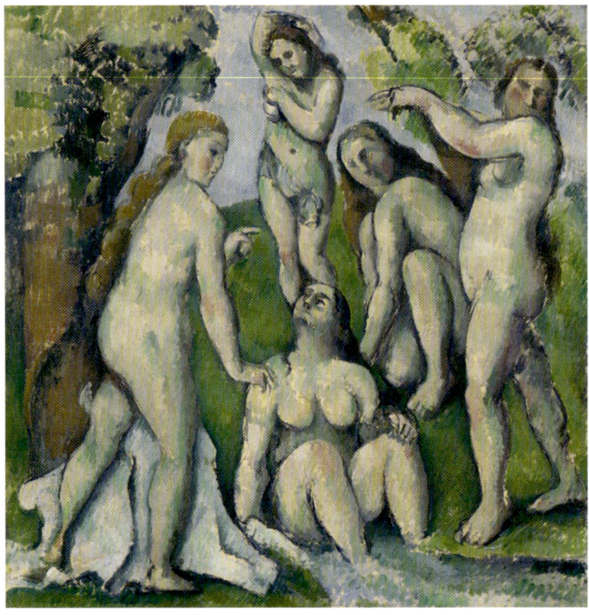

Paul Cézanne, *Five Bathers*, 1885/87
Oil on canvas, 65.3 × 65.3 cm
Kunstmuseum Basel, G 1960.1

Five women jostle for position in this preparatory sketch for
the larger painting of the same title, today in the Kunstmuseum
Basel (left, FWN 945). Groups of bathers in idealised Arcadian
landscapes were a theme that occupied Cézanne from the 1870s
until the end of his life. He produced nearly 200 scenes of this
subject, as paintings, drawings and prints (see cats 18–21).
Unlike his contemporaries who focused on bathing as an aspect
of modern life, Cézanne produced timeless scenes that owe more
to his predecessors, including Nicolas Poussin (1594–1655).

The figures dominate the square composition, their limbs
extending to the loosely sketched lines that frame it. Only a
curtain of foliage behind them alludes to their pastoral setting,
while their activity is made apparent only by the hurried strokes
at the bottom of the sheet, indicating the flowing waters of the
stream in which one bather sits. The two women behind her also
bathe, one crouching to reach the stream, the other standing to
wash herself. The woman at left holds a cloth, its sparsely drawn
drapery visible between her legs.

The women's poses – sitting, striding, crouching and
washing – betray Cézanne's sources. These are not live models
but antique sculptures. Cézanne copied figures from the Musée
du Louvre (see cats 11 and 15) and from reproductions (see cat.12),
adapting and distorting their stances in numerous paintings.
His technique of combining unrelated figures is evident in the
disconnection between his bathers. The hand of the woman at
left placed on the shoulder of the seated figure is a rare point of
interaction.

Uniquely for Cézanne, the sheet is squared to aid the artist
in transferring the composition to the larger canvas. This enhances the impression that all five women are in the foreground,
pressed up against the picture plane. This aspect, and the careful
balance of five poses, was appropriated by Pablo Picasso in *Les
Demoiselles d'Avignon* (1907, New York, Museum of Modern Art)
and by Henri Matisse in *La Danse* (1910, St. Petersburg, State
Hermitage Museum).

RMcK

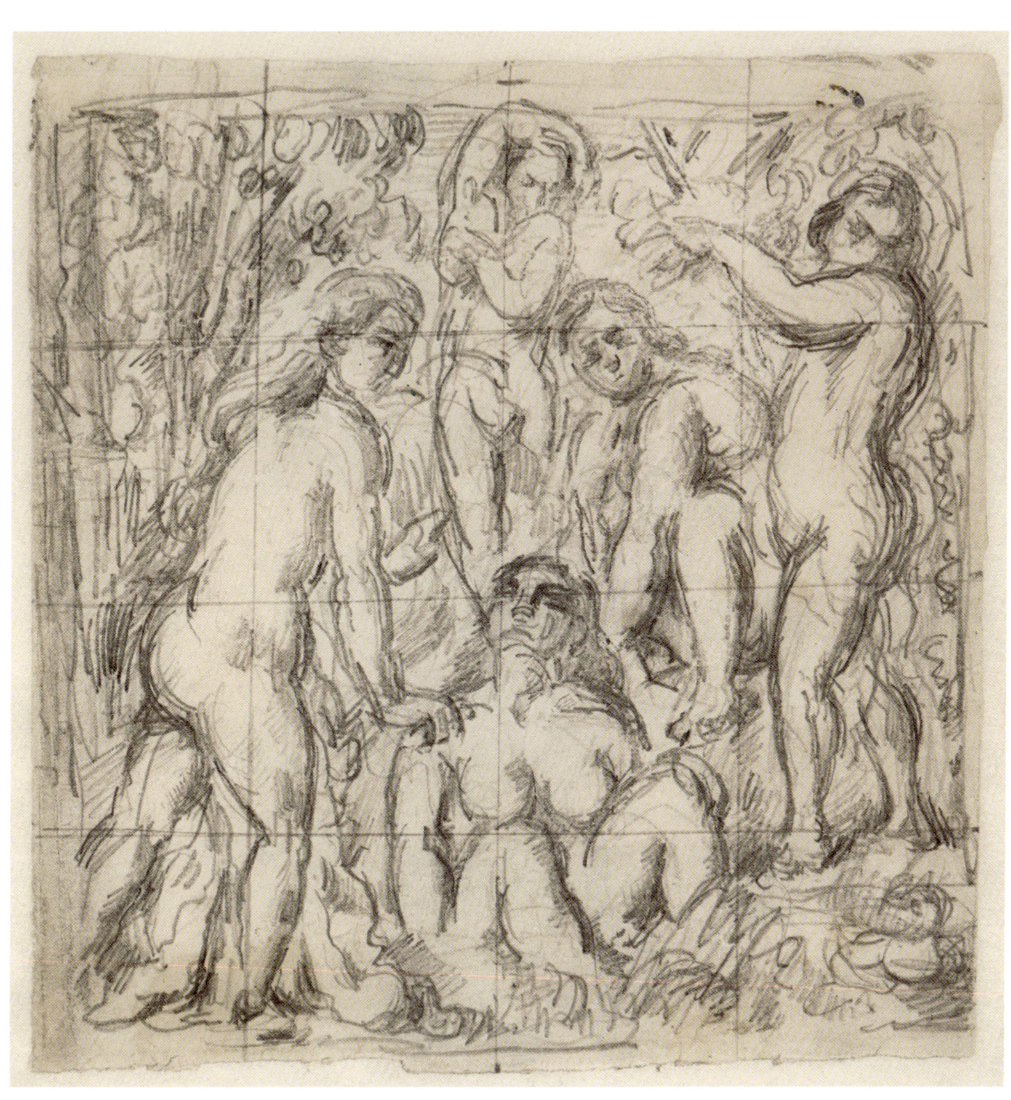

## 10

Paul Cézanne
*Victor Chocquet*, 1877–81

Pencil on paper, 9.5 × 8.6 cm
Chappuis 395; Feilchenfeldt/Warman/Nash 1727
Estate of Karsten Schubert, on extended loan to The Whitworth,
The University of Manchester

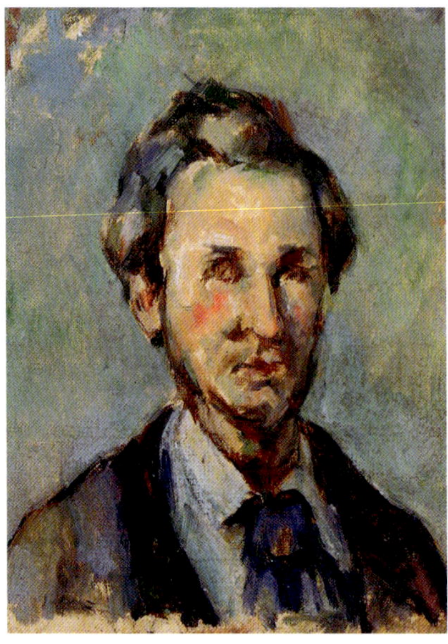

Paul Cézanne, *Portrait of Victor Chocquet*, c.1880
Oil on canvas, 20 × 15.5 cm
Simonow Collection, France

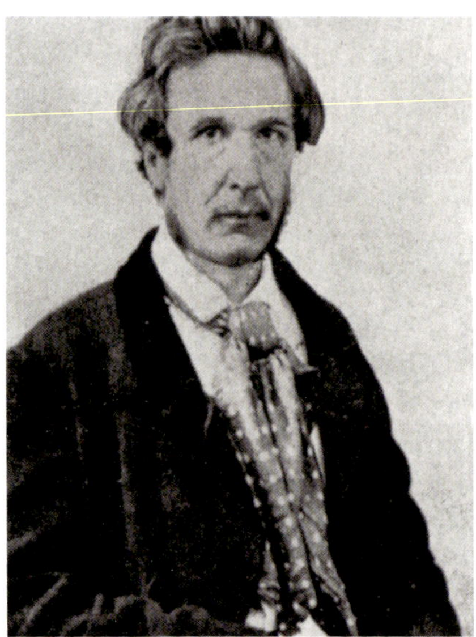

Photograph of Victor Chocquet, c.1860

This small but forceful portrait depicts Victor Chocquet
(1821–1891), one of Cézanne's most important patrons. The two
men were introduced in 1875 by Auguste Renoir and became
close friends. Chocquet had already begun collecting work by
the Romantic painter Eugène Delacroix, whom Cézanne greatly
admired. From 1875 Chocquet amassed a major collection of
Impressionist paintings by Renoir, Pissarro and Monet, plus
35 Cézannes. Among these were three of the six portraits of
Chocquet that Cézanne painted over 12 years.

In this drawing the artist carefully models his friend's
likeness – hatching the contours of his face and recognisable
quiff – and sketches in Chocquet's apparel. It is similar to a
depiction of the patron on another sheet of studies (FWN 2274,
collection of Jasper Johns). However, the pencil line framing
this drawing, and the initials at lower right, give it a sense of
containment and completion, raising the question of whether
it was executed from life or using another source.

Cézanne experimented with making portraits from
photographs in order to better understand the effect of the
sitter's physical presence. He owned a photograph of Chocquet
as a younger man, taken in about 1860, and used it to make
a painted portrait in 1880–85 (FWN 454, private collection),
greying his friend's hair for effect. In the present drawing the
sitter wears the same clothes as in that portrait, leading many
scholars to conclude that it too was made from the photograph.
However, in the drawing Chocquet appears older and has only
a whisper of the chinstrap beard present in the photograph.

This drawing is certainly connected to a small portrait –
only about twice this size – painted around 1880 (shown above
left, FWN 453) and formerly owned by another great Cézanne
collector, Auguste Pellerin (1853–1929). In the painting, the
pencil hatching becomes playful shading in blues and greens.
It has been argued that this earlier portrait was made from life,
while FWN 454 was based on the photograph, as the latter is
far more regimented in its brushstrokes.[1] By association, the
drawing would also be from life.

In comparing these images of Chocquet, it is not easy to
define the role of this sketch. A possibility yet to be explored
is that it was made from the earlier portrait (FWN 453). If this
were the case, Cézanne could here be using drawing to help him
transition between the youthful photograph and older portraits
of his friend.   RMcK

1  John Elderfield, *Cézanne Portraits*, Princeton University Press,
   Princeton, NJ, 2017, p.22.

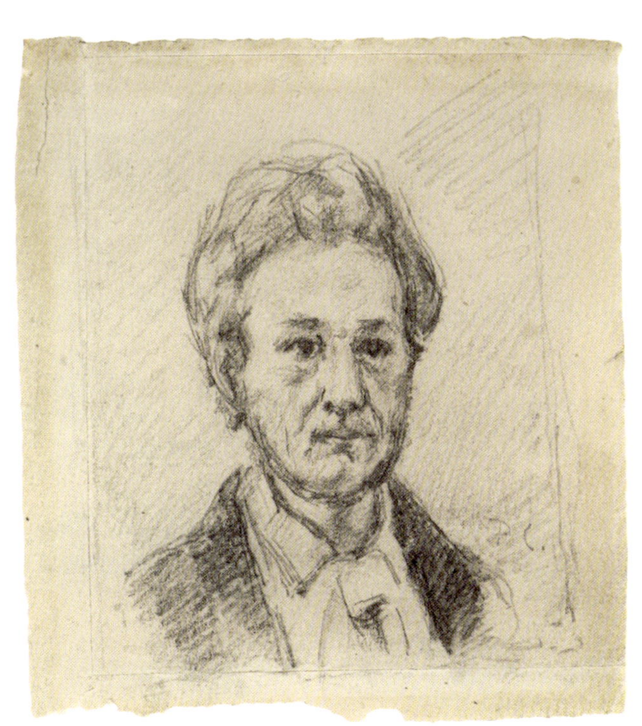

11

## Paul Cézanne

*After Pierre Puget: Milo of Croton*, c.1882–85

Pencil on paper, 19.6 × 12 cm
Venturi 1277; Chappuis 505; Feilchenfeldt/Warman/
Nash 3003-47a
Estate of Karsten Schubert, on extended loan to The Whitworth,
The University of Manchester

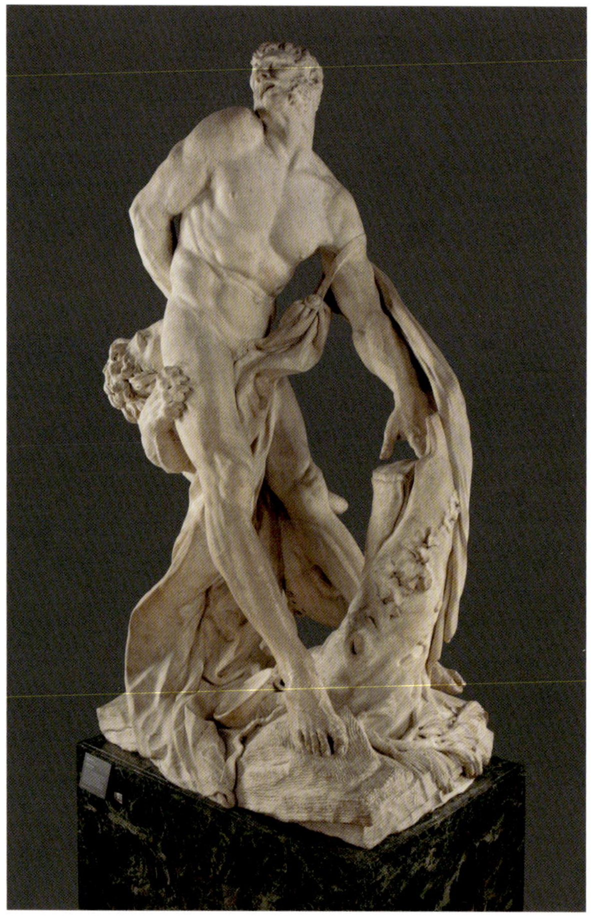

Pierre Puget, *Milo of Croton*, 1671–82
Marble, height: 270 cm
Musée du Louvre, Paris, MR 2075

This is one of 13 drawings Cézanne made from the 1683 marble sculpture *Milo of Croton* by Pierre Puget (1620–1694). The sketch is notable for the frenetic energy of the pencil marks, which capture the dynamism of the original sculpture showing the death of an Olympian athlete. Although ancient Greek sources describe the ageing Milo as being consumed by wolves after he hubristically attempted to cleave a tree stump in two, Puget depicts him devoured by a lone lion. Cézanne emphasises the protagonist's strength with rippling lines across the figure's tensed thigh, while repeated lines, building contrast, evoke the intensity of the lion's bite. Although an important part of the narrative, the drawing does not extend to Milo's hand caught in the tree stump.

When Cézanne first moved to Paris to train as an artist, he spent his afternoons copying in the Musée du Louvre. This drawing was made two decades later, when he continued to take inspiration from the museum's storehouse of figures. He drew from antique sculpture (see cat.15) as well as dynamic figures by Renaissance and Baroque sculptors. Cézanne was especially drawn to the work of Puget – a fellow Provençal artist and master of the surface tension to which he aspired. Cézanne made 18 sketches from his predecessor's more sedentary *Hercules Resting* (c.1663), also in the Louvre.

Cézanne sketched the *Milo of Croton* from a number of angles, but his sketchbooks are dominated by this viewpoint. The right profile of the sculpture focuses on the lion sinking its teeth into Milo's flesh and the zigzag of writhing limbs leading up to Milo's head as he throws it back in agony. Cézanne's repeated interrogation of the *Milo of Croton* from this angle might suggest that he was working from a photograph, but it would have had to be one that evoked the experience of looking up at the sculpture, which stands at 2.7 metres tall.

The inscription at lower left, XLVII, is a page number. This sheet was originally part of a sketchbook, today known as CP1 in reference to the great collector and connoisseur of Cézanne drawings Adrien Chappuis (1899–1979), who numbered these pages before dismantling the sketchbooks. At the top of this sheet, but not visible as mounted, is a list written in ink in the artist's handwriting, which begins 'Umbrella 8, Hat 12, Alcohol'.   RMcK

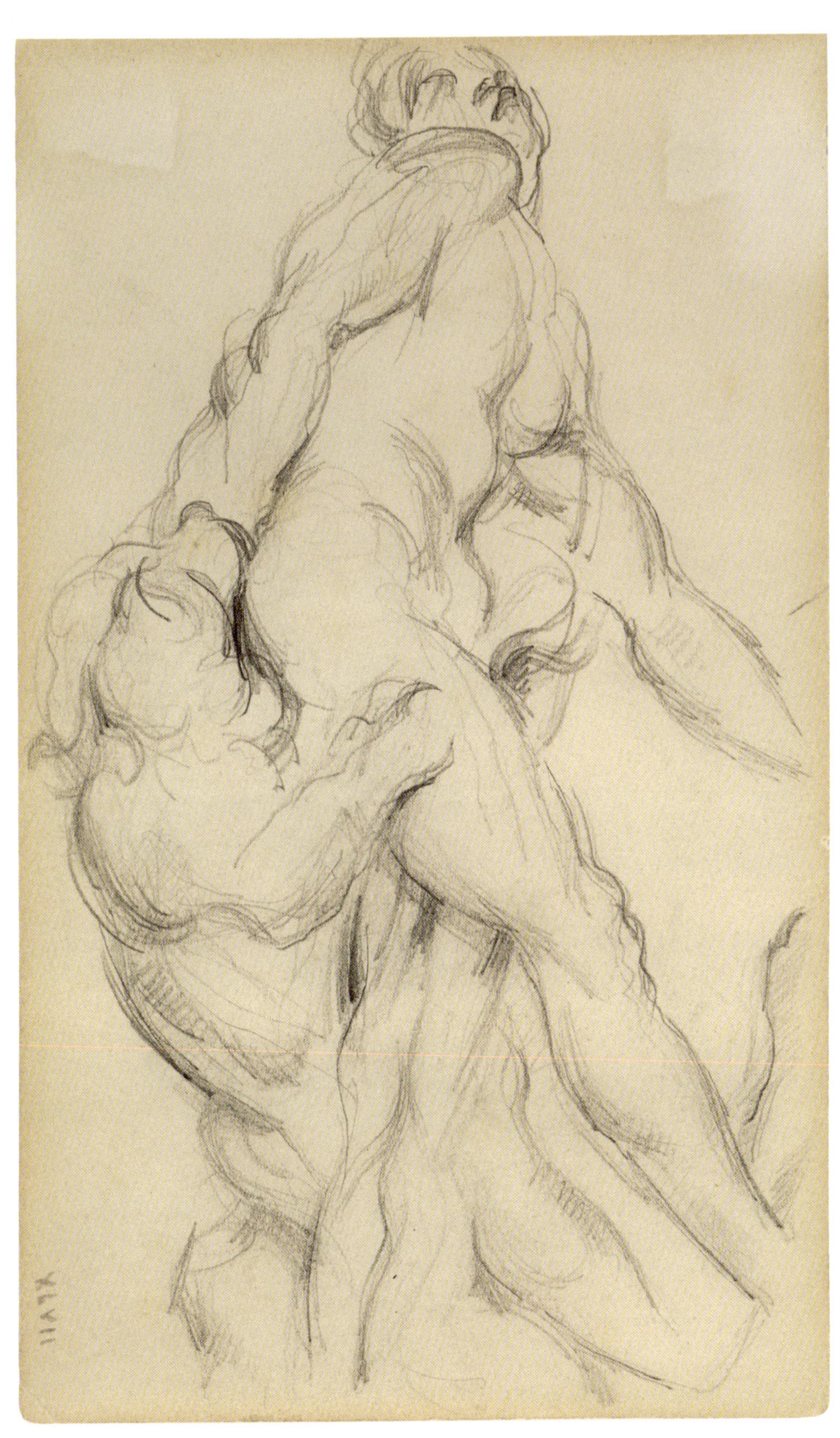

XLVII

12

Paul Cézanne

*Paul Cézanne Junior; Striding Bather; Head after Rubens, Ceres*, c.1882–83 and 1880

Pencil on paper, 22 × 12.5 cm
Venturi 1290-09; Chappuis 832; Feilchenfeldt/Warman/
Nash 3008-35b
Estate of Karsten Schubert, on extended loan to The Whitworth,
The University of Manchester

It was not unusual for Cézanne to make numerous unrelated studies on one page. This example is notable in containing four of the five subjects that dominate his sketchbooks, each at a different scale and orientation. In addition to the portrait, nude figure and copy from an Old Master on the recto, there is a landscape on the verso; a still life would complete the set.

The year 1877 is written at top right, but it is not in Cézanne's hand. The drawings on the recto were probably made on different occasions in the first years of the 1880s, and the landscape overleaf closer to the middle of the decade. This drawing came from the sketchbook known as CPII, which was already incomplete when it was bought by the Cézanne collector and connoisseur Adrien Chappuis from the art dealer Paul Guillaume.

The largest drawing on the recto is that of the head of the artist's son, Paul *fils*, here around ten years old. Cézanne swiftly outlines his facial features, modelling their forms with patches of fine hatching. Neatly arranged in differing directions, these carefully cast shadow on the left-hand side of his head.

Further down the sheet, where the boy's chest would be, is a melee of animated lines. At 90 degrees is a much smaller female head. It is Ceres, the Roman goddess of agriculture, copied after the Flemish Baroque painter Peter Paul Rubens, reportedly Cézanne's favourite painter. The 1615 original is in the State Hermitage Museum in St. Petersburg. Cézanne made his copy from an engraving published in 1879 in *Le Magasin pittoresque*, a periodical to which he referred repeatedly.

Turning the sheet a further 90 degrees, the nude seen from behind is not so easily sourced. The pose, striding forwards, arm outstretched, is a revenant that haunts Cézanne's sketchbooks. This pose appears on the left of numerous paintings of groups of bathers; the shading around her body in this drawing is indicative of the increasing lack of distinction between voluminous bodies and airy spaces in such scenes. Two canvases from the mid-1870s that feature this figure – both titled *Three Bathers* – were owned by Henry Moore (FWN 920, private collection) and Henri Matisse (FWN 923, Petit Palais, Musée des Beaux-Arts de la Ville de Paris). These two modern artists looked back to Cézanne's bathers with the same admiration he himself felt for Rubens's works.

RMcK

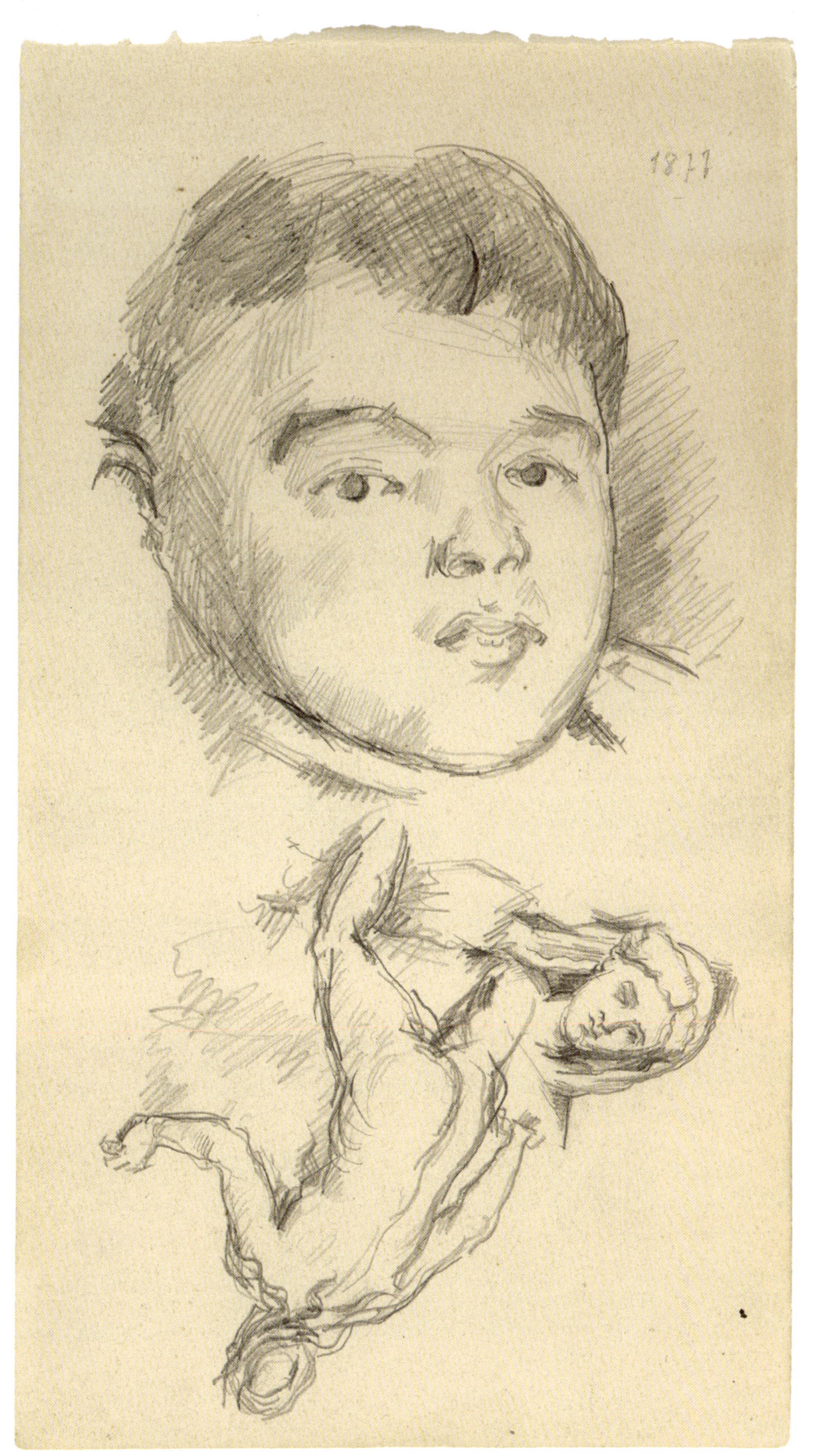
1877

13
Paul Cézanne
*Study of Heads: Paul Cézanne Junior Asleep and an Infant,*
c.1886–87

Pencil on blue paper, 12.4 × 21.5 cm
Venturi 1290; Chappuis 862; Feilchenfeldt/Warman/
Nash 3008-29b
Karsten Schubert Ltd., on loan to The Whitworth,
The University of Manchester

Cézanne's sketchbooks abound with images of his family –
especially his partner, Hortense Fiquet, whom he met at art
school in 1869, and their son, Paul, born in January 1872.
This drawing of his son (on the right) dates to a tumultuous
period in the artist's personal life. His longstanding friendship
with Émile Zola broke down a month before Cézanne married
Hortense on 28 April 1886. The couple's already strained
relationship disintegrated later the same year, following the
death of the artist's father, Louis-Auguste. The drawings of
Paul *fils* maintain a sense of paternal affection. By the age of 14
or 15, as in this drawing, the artist's son was a practised sitter
for both drawings and oil paintings.

The preponderance of drawings of Paul *fils* asleep, as here,
or absorbed in another activity such as reading, probably relates
to his father's insistence on his model's complete stillness.
When Cézanne's dealer Ambroise Vollard sat for his portrait,
the artist exclaimed: 'Do I have to tell you again you must sit like
an apple? Does an apple move?'[1] While some critics considered
Cézanne uninterested in the differences between the contours
of a head and those of an apple, the caring sketches of his son
suggest otherwise.

The other drawing on this sheet, the head of an unidentified
infant, is less developed. Just above it, a line indicates an aban-
doned first attempt at tracing the crown of the child's head.
The infant is seen from below at a challenging three-quarter
view. Cézanne carefully outlines the features, repeating strokes
on the right side of the face to build shadow.

A similar technique is used on the profile of Paul, but other
parts of his face are modelled with pencil hatching. Around the
back of the head and in the shadow of his collar the artist has
added indentations with a stylus or similar instrument. The
blue paper – a rarity among Cézanne's drawings – ensures the
contrast between light and shade is subtler than if it were on
a white support.

RMcK

1 Ambroise Vollard, *Paul Cézanne: His Life and Art*, trans. Harold L.
Van Doren, Crown Publishers, New York, 1937, p.76.

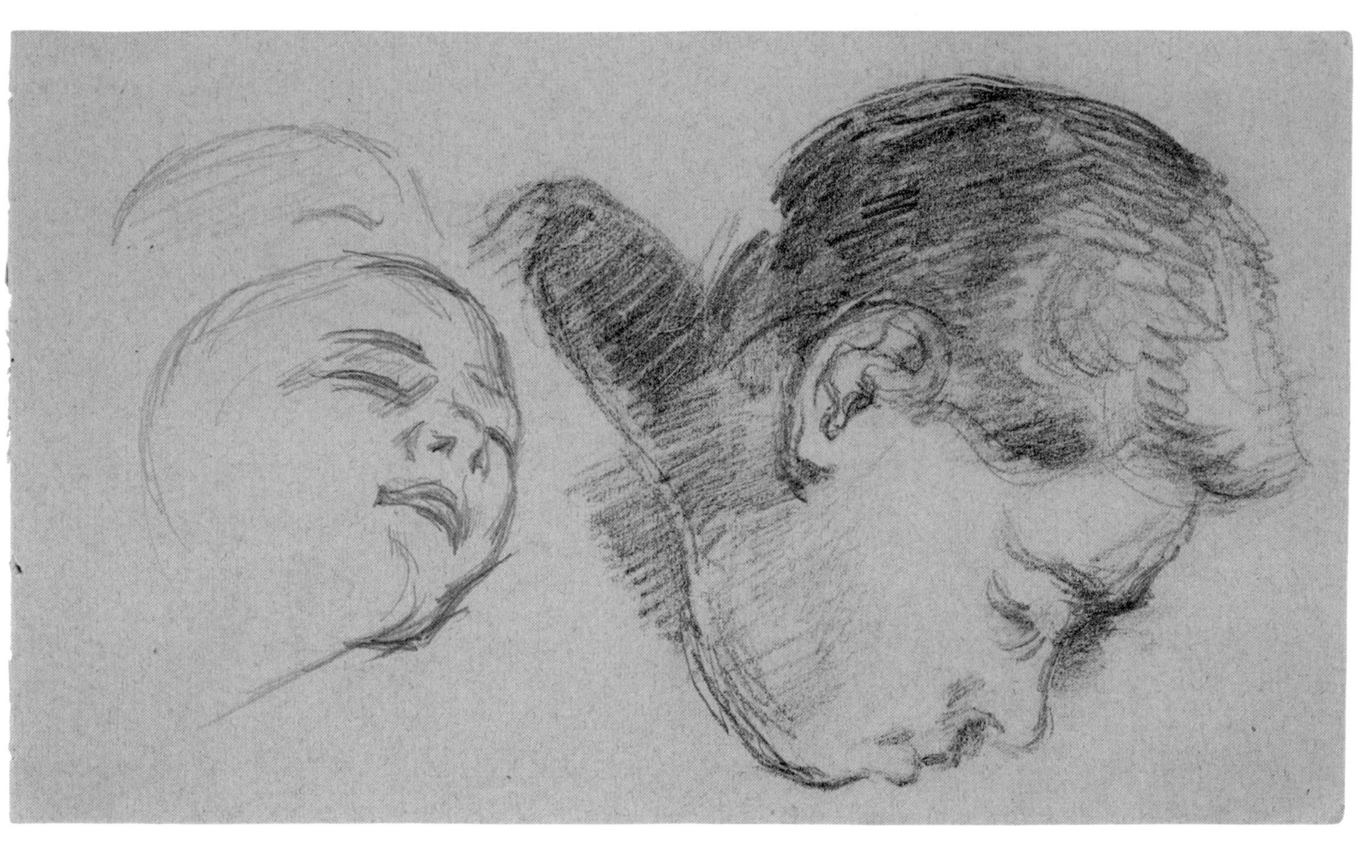

14

## Attributed to Paul Cézanne
*Skull*, c.1885–90

Pencil on paper, 14.5 × 15.2 cm
Rewald Watercolours (reverse) 278
Estate of Karsten Schubert, on extended loan to The Whitworth,
The University of Manchester

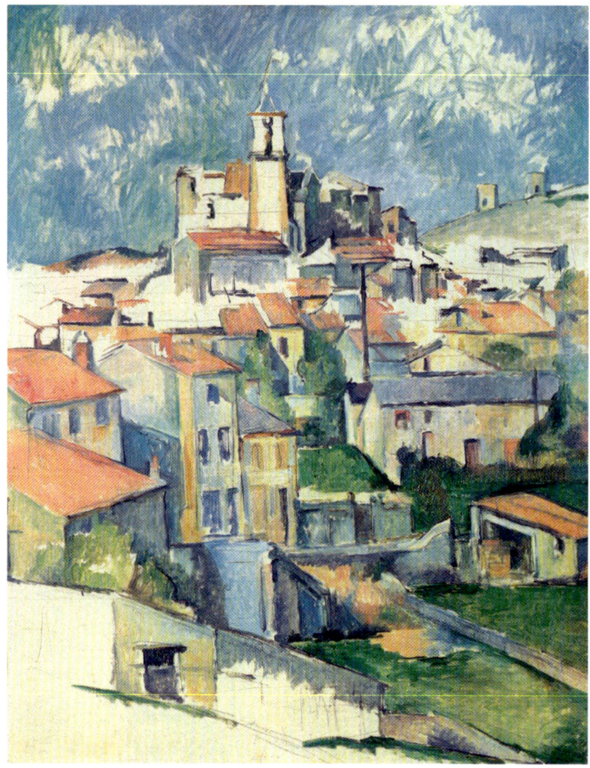

Paul Cézanne, *Gardanne*, 1885–86
Oil on canvas, 80 × 64.1 cm
Metropolitan Museum of Art, New York, 57.181
Gift of Dr. and Mrs Franz H. Hirschland, 1957

In 1905 Cézanne told his dealer Ambroise Vollard, 'A skull is
a beautiful thing to paint.'[1] In his late years, the artist kept three
examples in his Aix-en-Provence studio. Some skulls appear
in Cézanne's early drawings in a narrative context, but from
the 1880s they become increasingly present in his still lifes as
*memento mori*. This drawing, published for the first time here,
is not connected to any of those oil or watercolour paintings.

This sheet was previously known only for the watercolour
study of trees in Provence on the recto – the reason for the water
stains across the verso. That watercolour shares its subject, and
to an extent the interest in depicting depth and flatness, with
the *Study of Trees (La Lisière)* of about 1895 (cat.16). However, the
present sheet is more closely connected to a study of trees in the
Harvard Art Museums that dates to the second half of the 1880s
(FWN 1212). Although on a larger sheet, the Harvard watercolour
is also square in composition.

There may be another Provençal scene on the verso: some
faint but meticulously drawn buildings appear at the bottom
of the sheet at 90 degrees. With a three-storey townhouse at left,
and multiple levels of buildings, they resemble the hill town of
Gardanne.[2] In 1885–86 Cézanne stayed with his parents at their
house at Jas de Bouffan near Aix, accommodating his young
family at an apartment at 27 cours Forbin in Gardanne, a short
distance to the south. He painted the landscapes and villages of
this area in oils as well as watercolours. He depicted Gardanne
in paintings today held in the Metropolitan Museum of Art and
the Brooklyn Museum in New York and the Barnes Foundation,
Philadelphia (FWN 222–24). The buildings on this sheet were
surely drawn before the skull.

The skull itself is positioned at the top right of the square
page, its right edge meeting that of the sheet, which may have
been cut down. It is drawn with care and modelled with a mosaic
of passages of neat hatching. These mirror Cézanne's painting
style of constructing an image from patches of colour.

RMcK

1  Ambroise Vollard, *Paul Cézanne: His Life and Art*, trans.
   Harold L. Van Doren, Crown Publishers, New York, 1937, p.111.
2  François Chédeville, email to the author, August 2019.

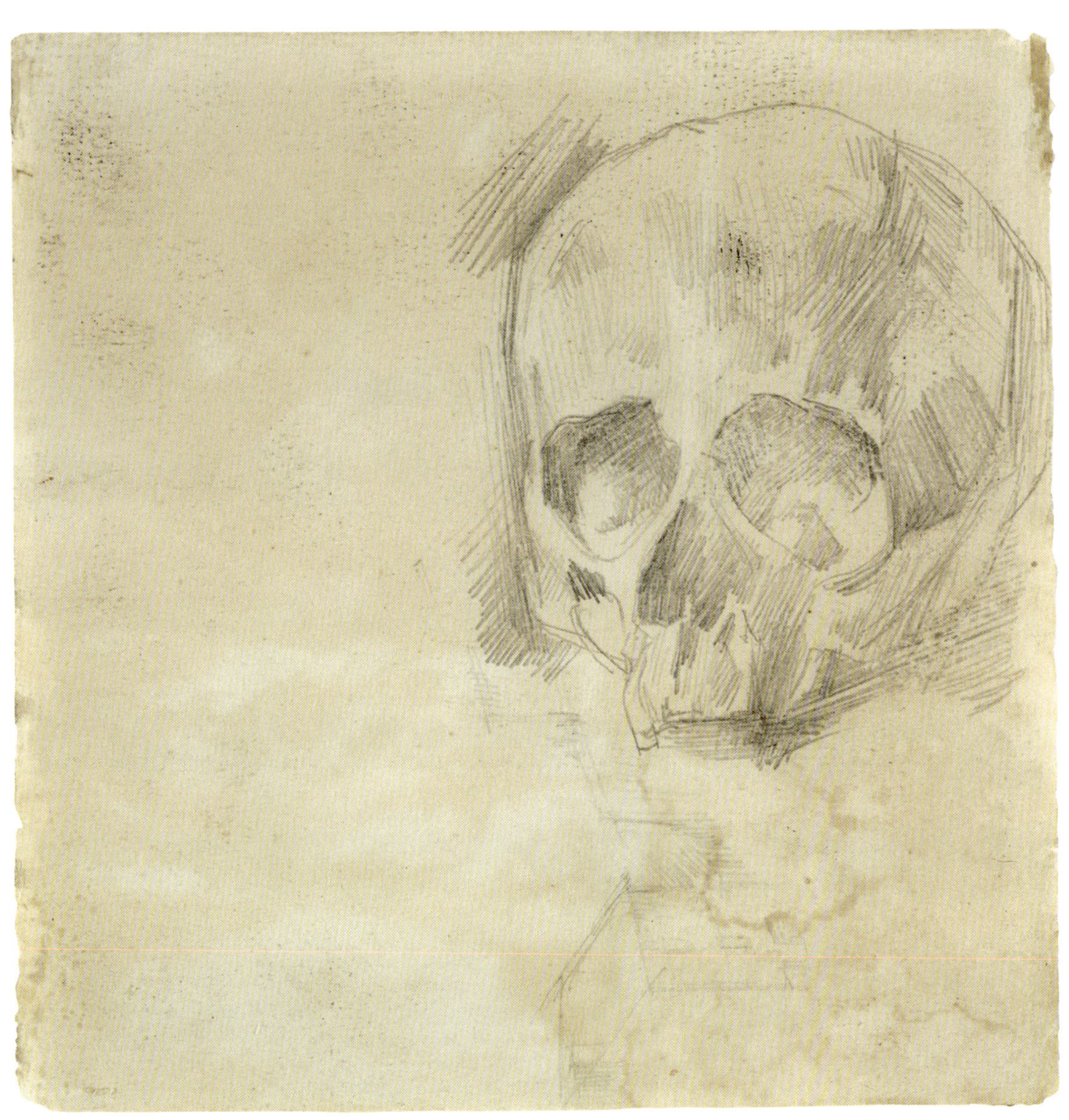

## 15

Paul Cézanne

*After the Antique: Crouching Venus*, c.1894–97

Pencil on paper, 19.6 × 12 cm
Venturi 1275; Chappuis 1098; Feilchenfeldt/Warman/
Nash 3003-42a
Estate of Karsten Schubert, on extended loan to The Whitworth,
The University of Manchester

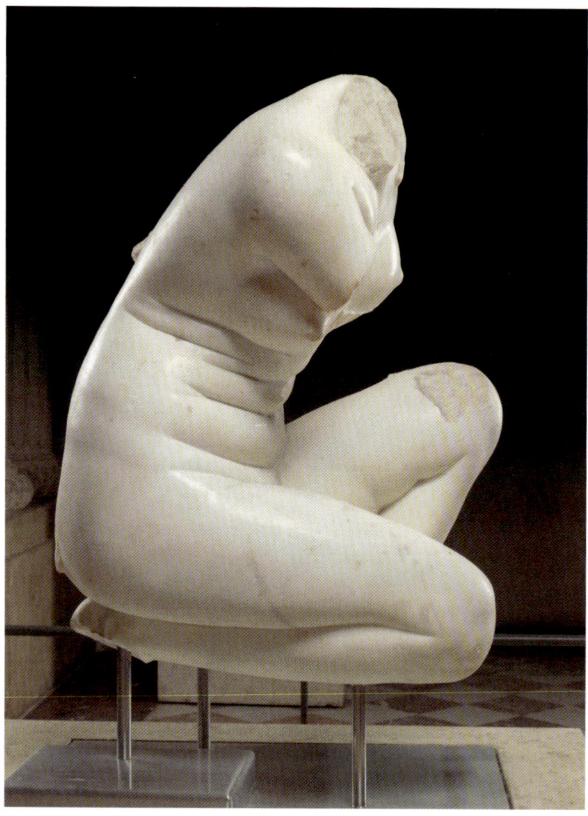

Roman, *Venus of Vienne*, 2nd century AD
Marble, height: 96 cm
Musée du Louvre, Paris

Cézanne repeatedly sketched the Hellenistic marble *Crouching Venus*, also known as the *Venus of Vienne* (second century AD). The sculpture was discovered in that city in 1878 and went on display at the Musée du Louvre the following year. Greek and Roman sculpture became part of the visual vocabulary of an artist who preferred not to draw from live models.

During his training as a draughtsman at the Aix-en-Provence School of Drawing in the late 1850s, Cézanne learnt to draw figures from plaster casts of antique statuary before graduating to the live nude. When he moved to Paris to continue his artistic training, he did the same in the city's museums. This was common among artists at the time, and Cézanne heeded and passed on the advice of the painter Thomas Couture to 'keep good company, that is, go to the Louvre'.[1] This drawing comes from the same sketchbook as that of the *Milo of Croton* (cat.11), also made in the Louvre, and has the later added page number XLII at top right.

The *Crouching Venus*, much like the 1686 sculpture on the same theme in the Louvre by Antoine Coysevox, provided Cézanne with voluptuous forms to copy. Typically for Cézanne, the sketch does not capture the whole sculpture. This is one of two very similar sketches of the sculpture; the other is found in the Philadelphia Museum of Art (FWN 3002-11b). In both he focuses on the profile of her crouched, leaning and gently twisting pose. He translates her form from three dimensions to two with an outline and then models the flesh of her breasts and belly. A deep shadow between her belly and thigh draws focus.

When sketching this sculpture from the other side – as seen in examples in the Kunstmuseum Basel (FWN 3005-09a) and the Louvre (FWN 3013-03a) – Cézanne included the restored arms, which have since been removed. This pose appears in multiple Cézanne compositions of bathing women: she reaches into the stream in *Five Bathers* (cat.9), and she is also at right in *Bathers, Small Plate* (cats 20–21).

On the verso of this drawing, at 90 degrees, is a frenetically sketched demon for the painting *The Temptation of Saint Anthony* (c.1877, Paris, Musée d'Orsay; FWN 650), one of many depictions of that subject made by Cézanne.   RMcK

1 Paul Cézanne, letter to Charles Camoin, 13 September 1903, in
  Alex Danchev (ed), *The Letters of Paul Cézanne*, Getty Publications,
  Los Angeles, 2016, n.228.

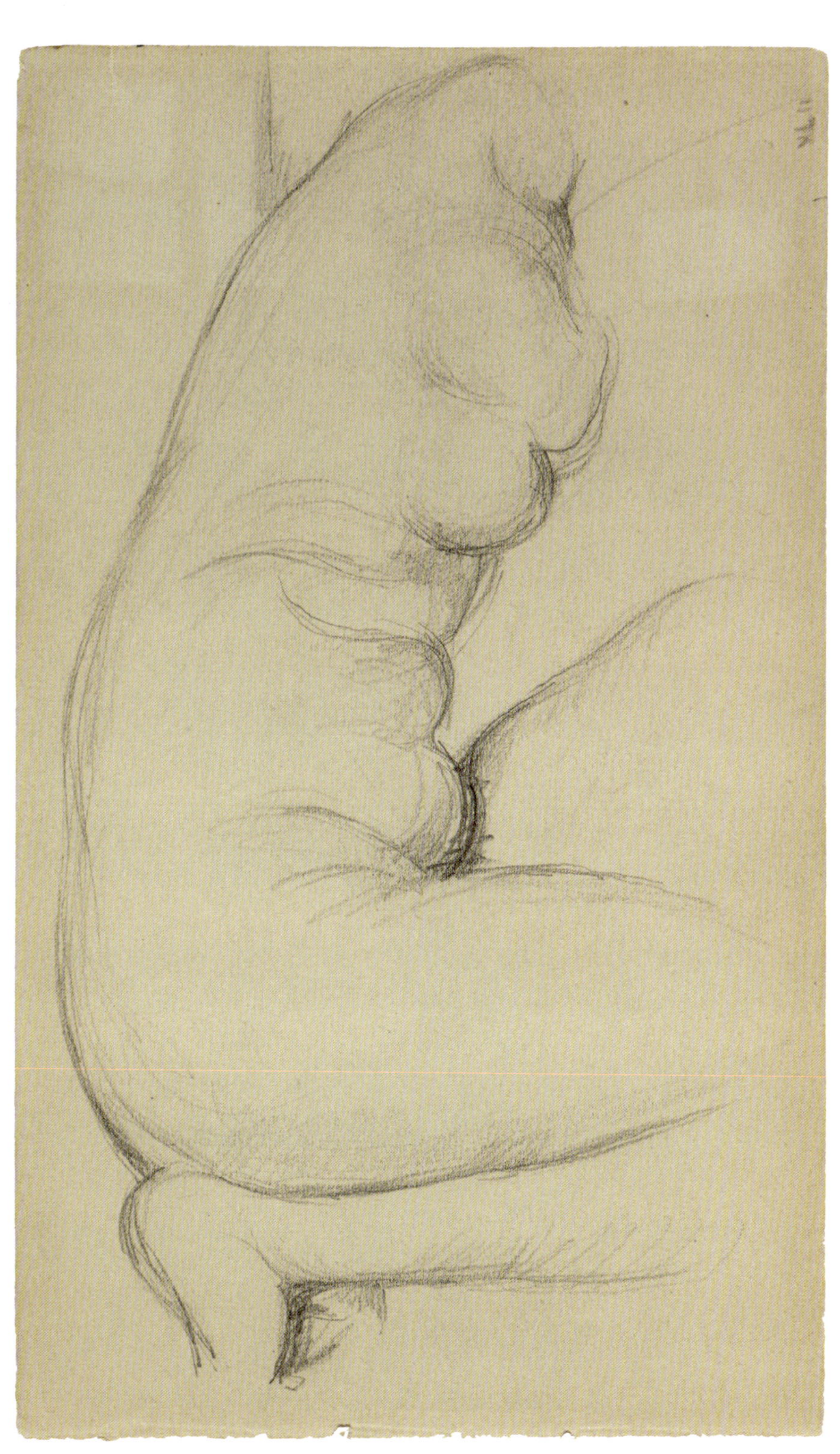

16
Paul Cézanne
*Study of Trees (La Lisière)*, c.1895

Pencil and watercolour on paper, 31.2 × 48.1 cm
Venturi 969; Rewald Watercolours 414; Feilchenfeldt/Warman/
Nash 1348
The Whitworth, The University of Manchester, D.1927.16
Purchased from the Leicester Galleries, London, 1927

Cézanne depicts trees and a thicket, one of his regular motifs
of the 1890s, with pencil and watercolour. It is a sparsely painted
work in which the artist shows little interest in the canopy
or foreground, instead developing the trunks. Subject and
approach converge as he depicts the edge (*lisière*) of a forest and
experiments with the two-dimensional representation of spatial
depth, one of his key pictorial concerns.

Areas of mossy green, yellows and greys across the sheet,
combined with thick pencil shading, evoke the distinctive
patches of short strokes that cover the surface of Cézanne's
canvases. A rectangle of sky blue overlaps with the trees, creating
a sense of airiness where we expect a dense wood. Calligraphic
black watercolour adds definition to the trunks at left and the
surface of the ground to the right. It does not, however, suggest
any shadow between and beyond the trees deeper into the forest.
As a result, this bright scene, seemingly bleached by sunshine,
appears resolutely flat on the paper's surface.

This flatness is a feature of many landscapes Cézanne painted
in his native Aix-en-Provence. The subject of undergrowth and
wooded areas also caught his attention on a trip to the resort
of Talloires in Haute-Savoie in July 1896, where he painted Lake
Annecy. The forest depicted in this work could well be Alpine
rather than Provençal. The comparison to other sparse studies
of trees does not aid in placing this sheet. Another watercolour
of this motif on a very similar paper size and with the same
watermark, 'CF' in a shield (here at top right), in the Museum
Boijmans Van Beuningen, Rotterdam (FWN 1282), has been
linked to this sheet.

The Whitworth bought this large watercolour in 1927.
Private collectors in the United Kingdom had begun to acquire
works by Cézanne in the 1910s and 1920s. This was the third
Cézanne to enter a public institution, and the first outside
London.[1]

RMcK

1  Richard Thomson, *French 19th Century Drawings in the Whitworth Art
   Gallery*, exh. cat., Whitworth Art Gallery, Manchester, 1981, p.8.

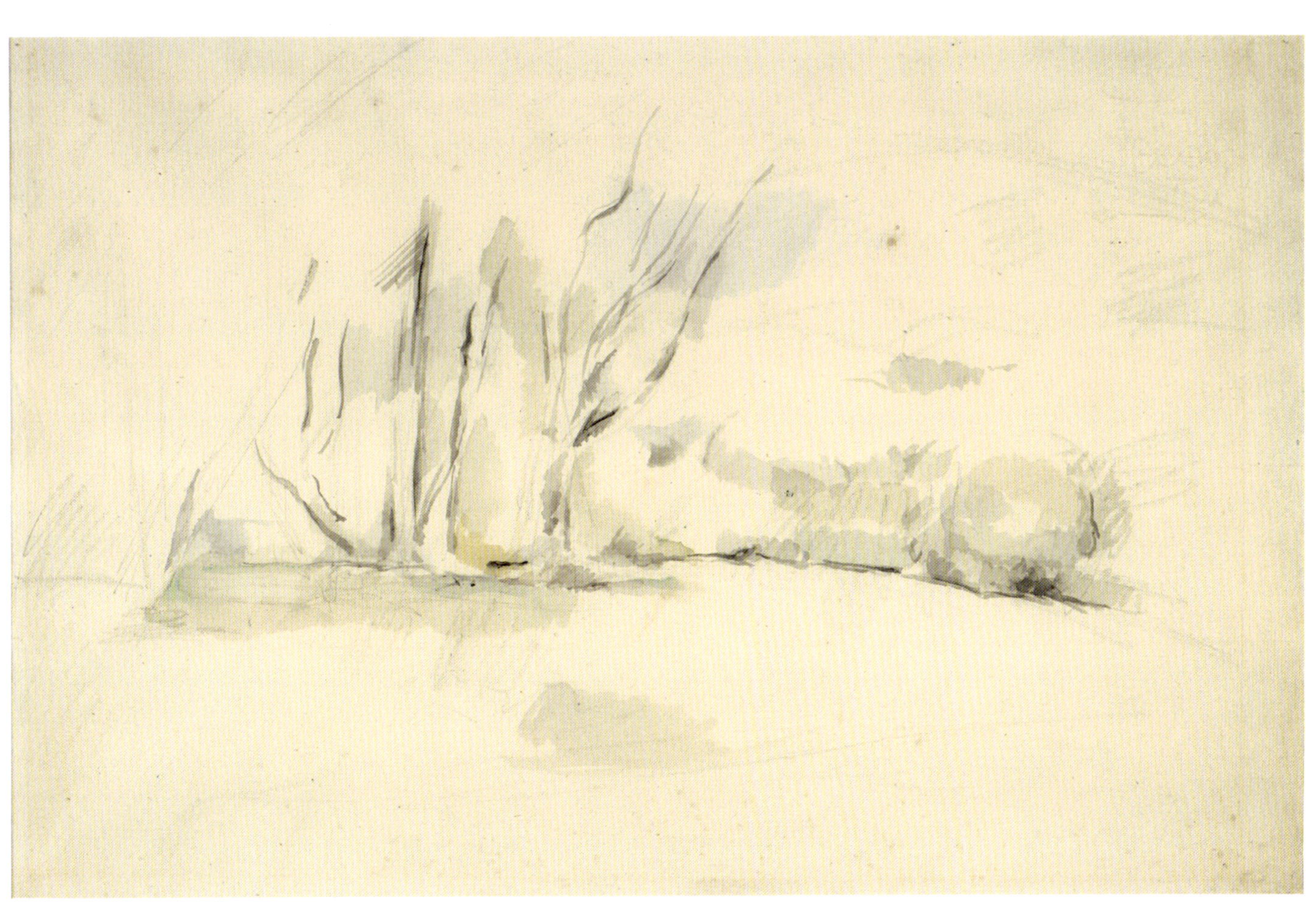

17
Paul Cézanne
*Self-portrait*, 1896

Lithograph (in black), 62.2 × 48.9 cm (sheet)
Venturi 1158; Cherpin 8
The Whitworth, The University of Manchester, P.2019.5
Karsten Schubert, gift 2019

Over 20 years after his first foray into printmaking (see cats 4–7) Cézanne produced three lithographs, including this self-portrait. He was asked to do so by the dealer Ambroise Vollard, an advocate of printmaking among painters and who gave Cézanne his first one-man show in 1895. This large self-portrait print would have promoted the artist and his work in tandem.

Unfamiliar with lithography, Cézanne drew this image on a special paper, and the printer transferred it to the lithographic stone. Had Cézanne drawn directly onto the stone the image would be reversed. Tellingly, the artist appears turned to the right, as in the majority of his painted self-portraits.

Cézanne, now in his late fifties, had drawn and painted himself throughout his life. His distinctive dark eyes are here emphasised by the bold monochrome. He wears a familiar heavy jacket, and a beret that also appears in a painted portrait (FWN 529, Museum of Fine Arts, Boston). His bow tie is partially obscured by his curving moustache and goatee beard.

Unusually for Cézanne, he includes a tool of his trade. The rectangle cutting across the right of the sheet has been identified as a canvas or drawing block, but given the medium it could be a portfolio. It occupies a similar position to the stretched canvas in the artist's painted self-portrait holding a palette (1886–87, Zurich, Foundation E.G. Bührle Collection; FWN 499).

There exists a maquette of this print heightened with watercolour (Ottawa, National Gallery of Canada), but it is complete in monochrome. Vollard had his printer Auguste Clot make editions of this work after the artist's death. An edition was begun in 1914 but was interrupted by the First World War, and one in black was produced in 1920. A watermark at right on this impression identifies the paper manufacturer Canson & Montgolfier France and at bottom left the paper stock Ingres.
RMcK

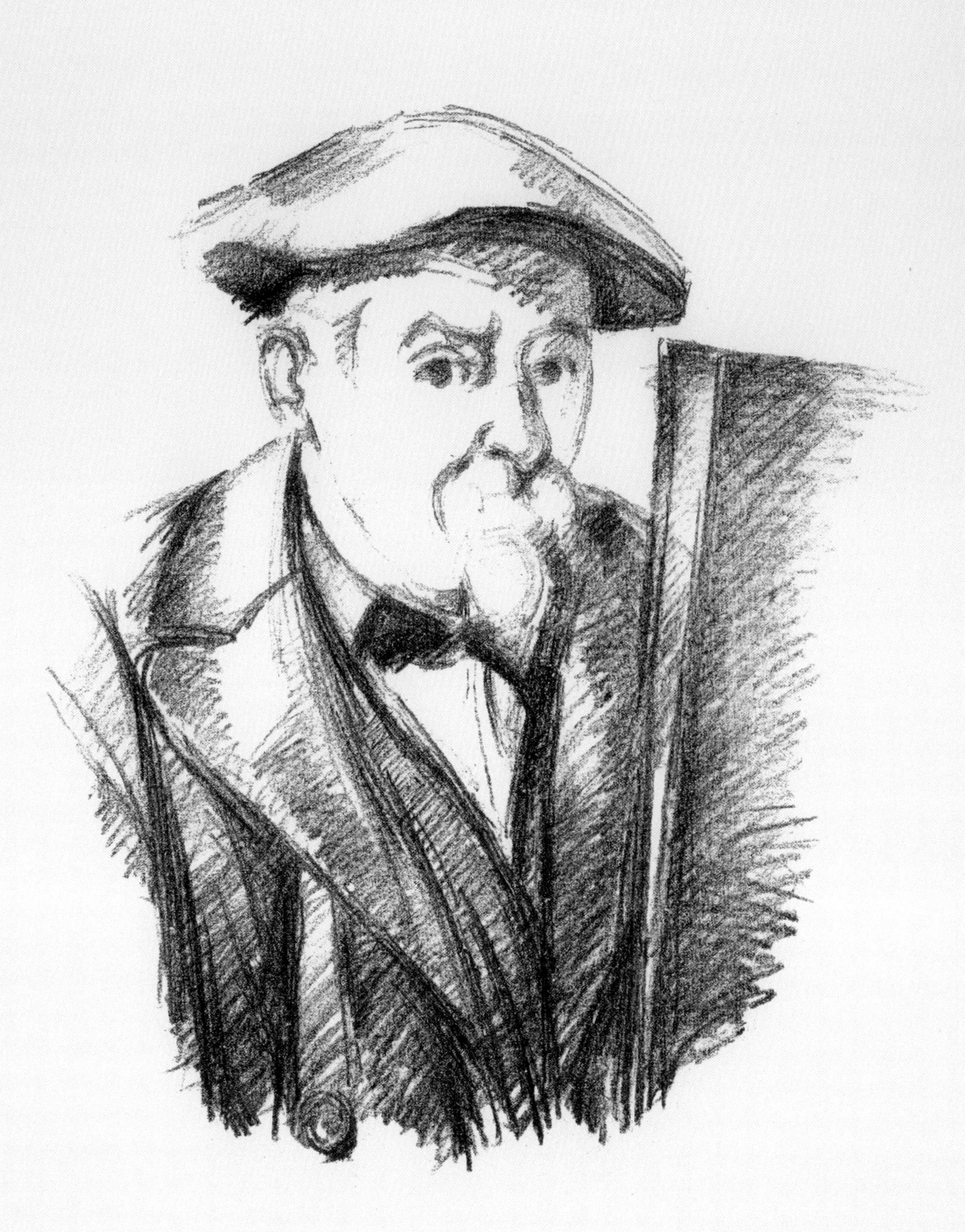

18

Paul Cézanne

*Bathers (Large Plate)*, 1896–98

Lithograph (first state of three), 40.1 × 50 cm (image);
48 × 62 cm (sheet)
Venturi 1157; Cherpin 7
Estate of Karsten Schubert, on extended loan to The Whitworth,
The University of Manchester

Bathers were an important subject in Cézanne's work from the 1870s onwards (see cat.9). When asked by his dealer Ambroise Vollard to make lithographs, Cézanne repeated a composition from a painting of four bathers made two decades previously. The artist's reputation was growing in this period, and given the opportunity to disseminate his work to a larger audience, Cézanne chose bathers (see also cats 20–21) in front of the Montagne Sainte-Victoire. The arrangement of figures in space and the production of a print from a painting are reminiscent of Marcantonio Raimondi's *The Judgment of Paris* (cat.1).

The decision to reproduce *Bathers at Rest* (FWN 926, below) may be indicative of the notoriety of this painting in the 1890s, many years after it was first shown in the third Impressionist exhibition of 1877. Vollard displayed this work in the window of his gallery during his 1895 Cézanne exhibition. Two years later, *Bathers at Rest* was included among the works to be donated to the French government by the Impressionist painter Gustave Caillebotte. *Bathers at Rest* and another Cézanne were rejected by the state. However, the probability that the artist made the black version of this lithograph in 1896 precludes it from being a response to the events of 1897.[1]

The lithograph exists in three states: the black keystone print (cat.18), the final colour lithograph (cat.19) and an intermediary colour phase. The artist created the black and colour versions in two stages. First Cézanne would have drawn the composition on transfer paper, which the printer Auguste Clot made into a printing stone. Cézanne then painted watercolour onto black-ink impressions made from that stone. Clot used these as a guide to prepare the six colour stones (ochre, blue, orange, green, yellow, red), a process that interested Cézanne.

This process supports the complex interaction between black and colour in this print. Cézanne used colour, especially blue, to model the line drawings of bathers made in black. The wisps of black in the sky that contour the clouds, created with shades of taupe and blue-grey, show the forethought of an artist for whom colour and line were usually integrated.

The final colour print was published as an edition of 100, as per the inscription at the bottom. The laid paper gives the feeling of a unique work, amplified by the conspicuous watermark 'MBM', which appears both above and below the image.   RMcK

1   Douglas Druick, 'Cézanne's Lithographs', in William Rubin (ed),
    *Cézanne: The Late Work*, Museum of Modern Art, New York, 1977, p.130.

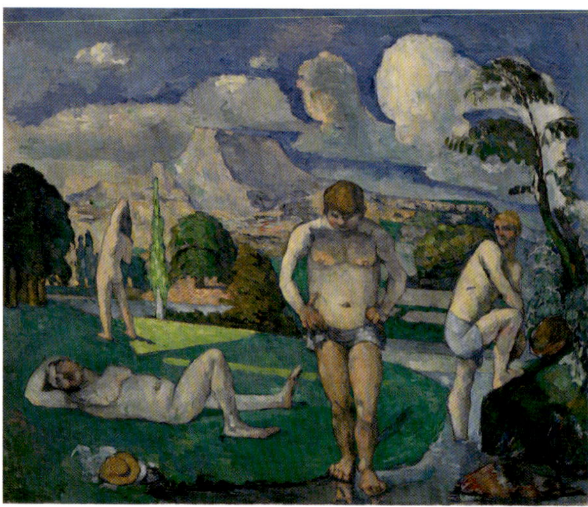

Paul Cézanne, *Bathers at Rest*, 1876–77
Oil on canvas, 82.2 × 101.2 cm
Barnes Foundation, Philadelphia, BF906

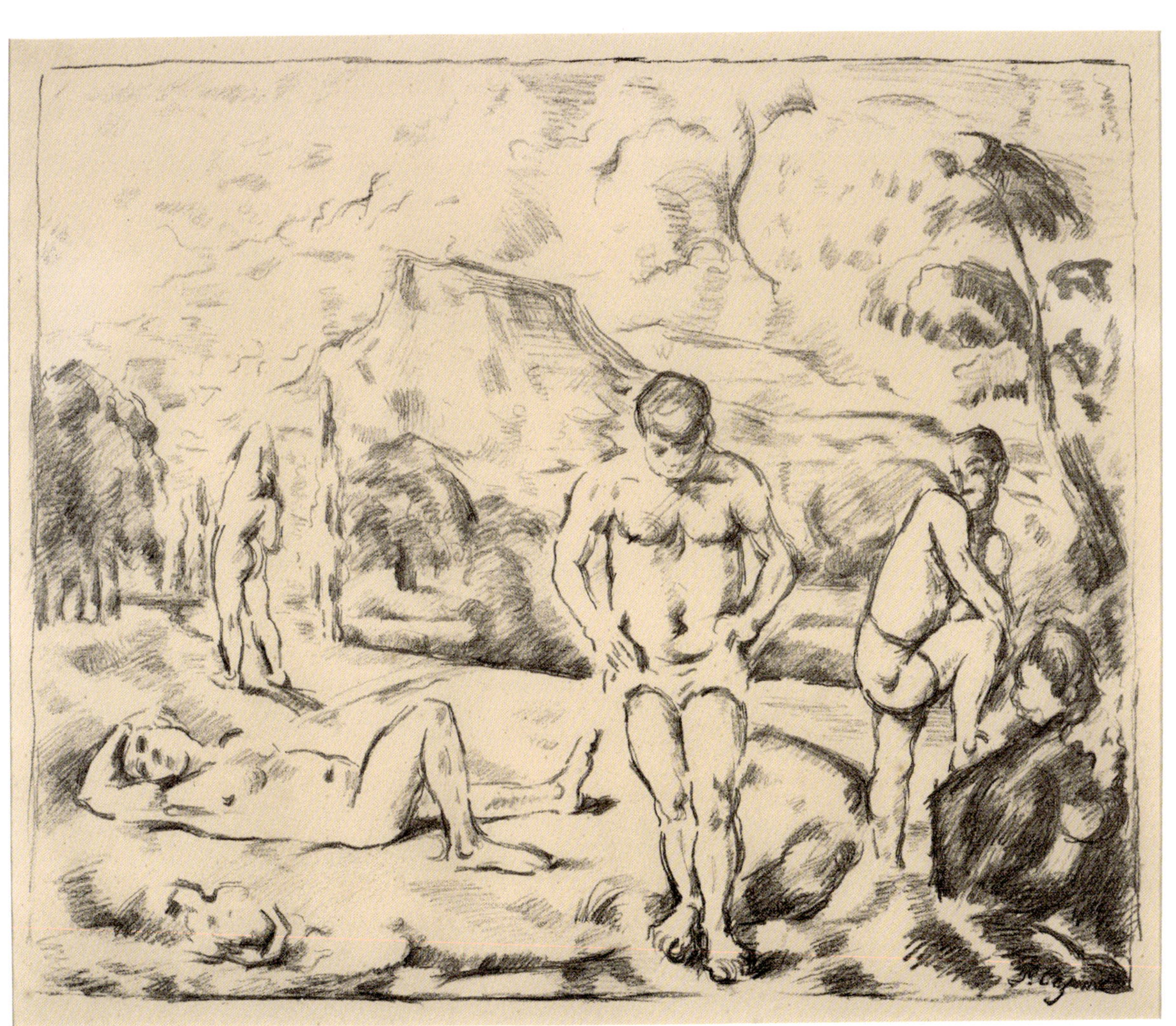

19
Paul Cézanne
*Bathers (Large Plate)*, 1896–98

Colour lithograph (third state of three),
40.1 × 50 cm (image); 48 × 62 cm (sheet)
Venturi 1157; Cherpin 7
The Whitworth, The University of Manchester, P.2019.6
Karsten Schubert, gift 2019

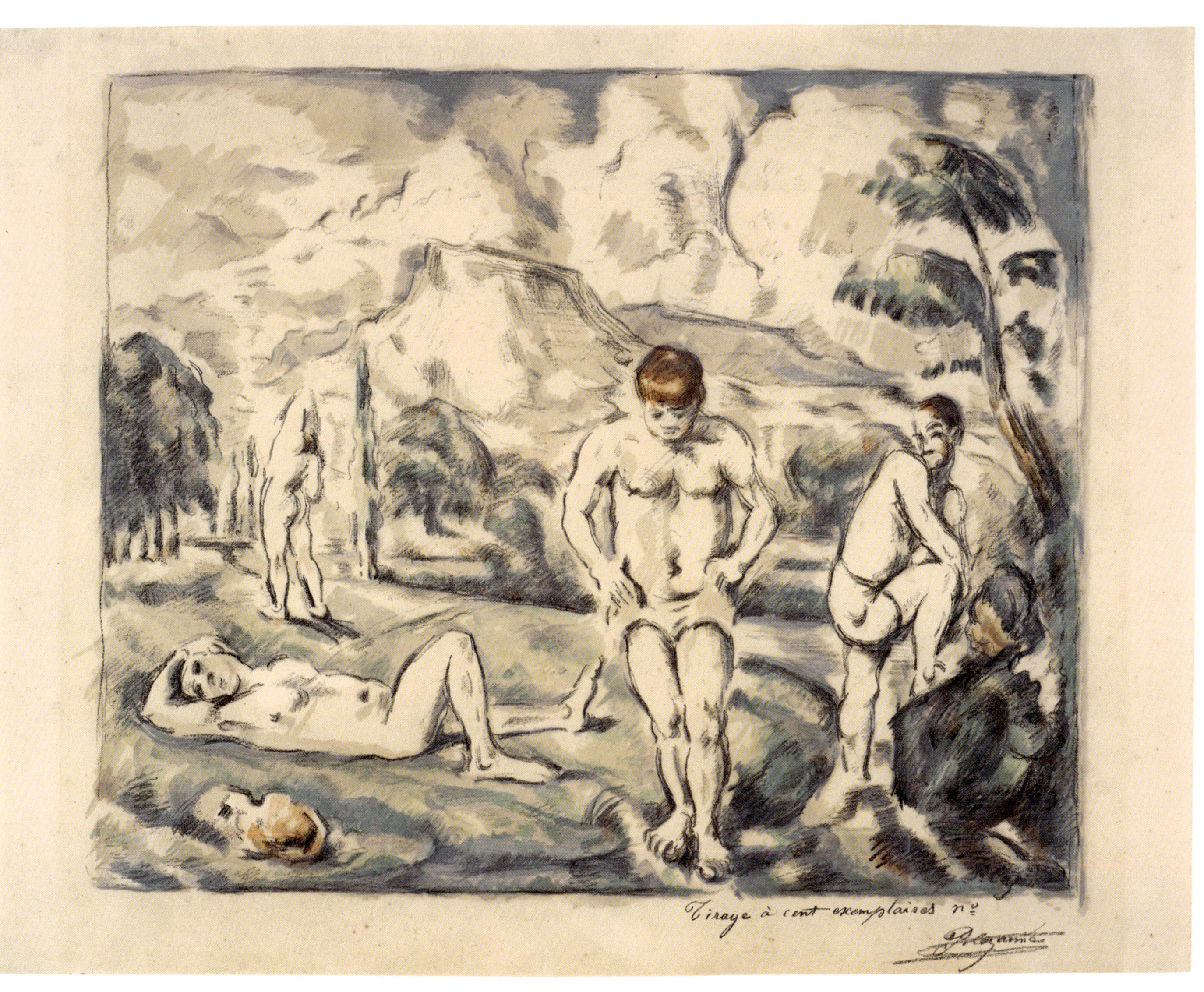

Tirage à cent exemplaires nº
P. Cézanne

20

Paul Cézanne

*Bathers (Small Plate)*, 1896–97

Colour lithograph (first state of two),
23.5 × 29 cm (plate); 29.4 × 36 cm (sheet)
Cherpin 6
The Whitworth, The University of Manchester, P.2018.1
Karsten Schubert, gift 2018

This is the only one of Cezanne's three lithographs to be published as part of an album. His dealer Ambroise Vollard included
it – with the title *Le Bain* – in *La Deuxième Année de l'Album
d'estampes originales de la galerie Vollard* of December 1897. It was
probably begun after the *Self-Portrait* and *Bathers (Large Plate)*
(cats 17–18) as the artist drew directly onto the lithography
stone, rather than using transfer paper. This may reflect his
increasing willingness to experiment with lithography, under
the encouragement of Vollard and the printer Auguste Clot.
It also dates the creation of the first state to Cézanne's presence
in Paris before April 1897.[1]

Cézanne's lack of experience with this technique is evident
in the accomplished draughtsman's uneasy lines. The drawing
and composition are simpler than in *Bathers (Large Plate)*. When
creating a maquette in watercolour, from which Clot could make
the stones for the second state in colour, Cézanne gave colours
a more active role in the composition. Blue, green and yellow
differentiate the foliage from the sky and articulate the grassy
knoll on which two bathers sit, which is only implied by the
areas of cast shadow articulated in black.

Typically for Cézanne, the six bathers – two standing, three
sitting and one submerged to his waist in a pool – are closely
clustered but do not interact. At either side they are framed by
trees, which are a common feature of his bathing scenes. The
composition relates to numerous painted groups of bathers
from the early 1890s. However, it is closest to *Group of Seven
Bathers* (c.1900, Riehen/Basel, Fondation Beyeler; FWN 973),
which has an additional figure in the water. That canvas has
previously been dated to the 1880s but may in fact be from 1900
and made after this print.

The colour lithograph in the Whitworth collection (cat.21)
dates from a second edition of *Bathers (Small Plate)* made by
Vollard in 1914, eight years after Cézanne's death. This was given
to the gallery in 1926, the first Cézanne print to enter a British
public collection.

RMcK

1 Douglas Druick, 'Cézanne's Lithographs', in William Rubin (ed),
  *Cézanne: The Late Work*, Museum of Modern Art, New York, 1977, p.127.

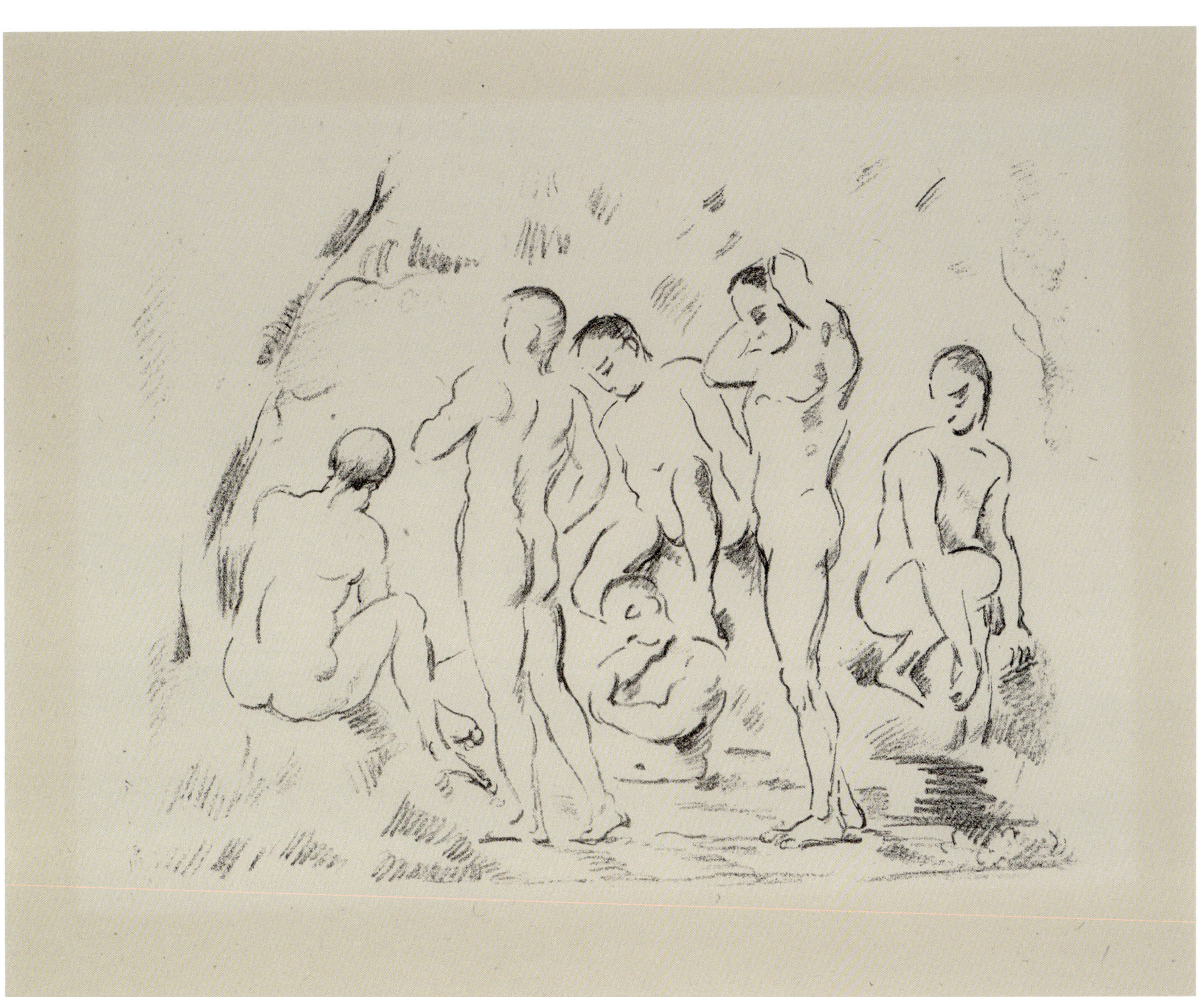

21

Paul Cézanne

*Bathers (Small Plate)*, 1896–97

Colour lithograph (second state of two),
23.5 × 29 cm (plate); 29.4 × 36 cm (sheet)
Cherpin 6
The Whitworth, The University of Manchester, P.4942
Presented by Victor Rienaecker through The Art Fund, 1926

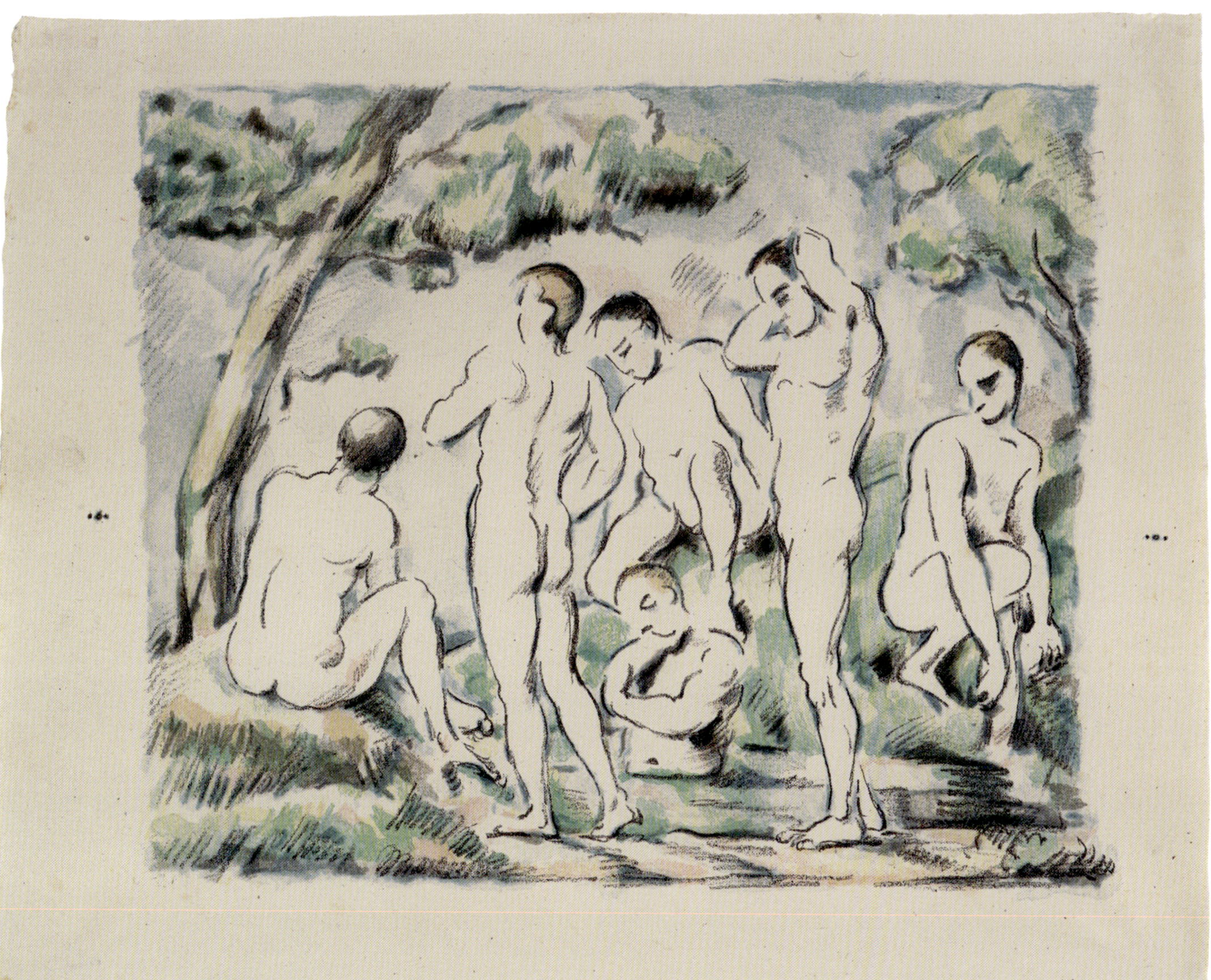

22

Pablo Picasso

*Untitled [Two Bathers and Playing Child, after Manet's
'Le Déjeuner sur l'herbe'], 1961*

Inscribed top left: '6.6.61 VI/Picasso'
Pencil on paper, 33 × 50.2 cm
Zervos XX.20
Private Collection, on loan to The Whitworth,
The University of Manchester

This is the sixth of eleven drawings with the same imagery that
Pablo Picasso executed on 6 June 1961. At the exact midpoint
of the series, it is the most simplified of all. The voluptuous
bulk of the two women – one hunched and active, the other
reclining languidly – is conjured merely by firm contours and a
few deft marks denoting essential bodily details. The crawling
child seems barely human, as if still at an amoeboid stage.
In the other drawings the setting is evoked in greater detail,
indicators of spatial recession are introduced and the child
acquires characteristics. Here, Picasso opted for the minimalist
biomorphic style he had practised during the 1920s when he
was close to the Surrealists. As for the toy train, it might almost
have been drawn by a child.

Stemming from a monochrome painting finished the
previous day, the drawings were made at a turning point in
Picasso's career. A few days later, he and his wife Jacqueline
moved from their villa in Cannes to a secluded farmhouse in
nearby Mougins, where he would spend the rest of his life.
With its peaceful, quasi-Arcadian imagery, the series served as
a fantasised escape from the bedlam of the imminent move.
It may also have involved nostalgia for the years Picasso spent
in Vallauris with Françoise Gilot and their two small children,
whom he had often portrayed playing with their toys. Another
significant connection is with the diverse body of works inspired
by Manet's *Le Déjeuner sur l'herbe* (1863) that had occupied Picasso
between August 1959 and July 1960. The woman drying her
foot recalls the crouching bather in the background of Manet's
masterpiece, and within days of the move Picasso had embarked
on a new spate of variations: the drawings were his route back
to that intense but temporarily shelved creative dialogue.

EC

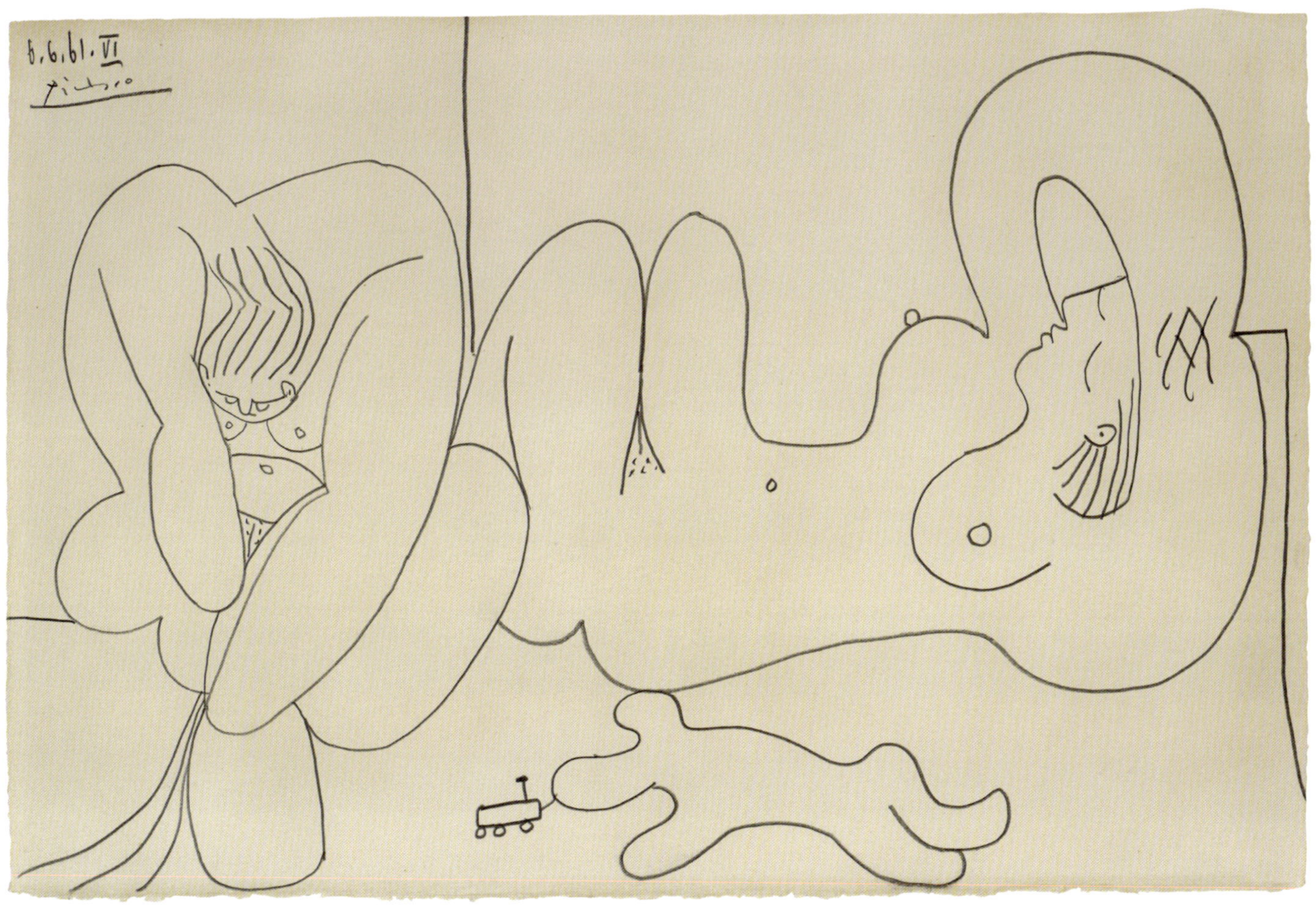

23
Michael Landy
*Self-Portrait No. 1*, 2008


Pencil on paper, 70 × 50 cm
Karsten Schubert Ltd., on loan to The Whitworth,
The University of Manchester

In 2007–8 Michael Landy executed a series of 70 portrait
drawings of family and friends, each one 70 by 50 centimetres.
The idea for the series came after the artist had made this self-
portrait, which became a kind of template for both the style
and execution of the subsequent works. All the drawings take
the same form, with only the head itself represented; the neck
is never shown, and nor is there any extraneous detail such as
elements of the room in which the subjects sat for their portrait.
The resultant images seem to float in space.

Drawn with a fine, sharp pencil, each portrait took two days
to make, with about eight hours of work each day. They are
extraordinarily finely wrought, with each wrinkle and crease
represented. Bristles, moles and other imperfections are all
given the same attention as noses, ears or eyebrows. Landy has
described these drawings as 'a kind of inventory' of the features
and peculiarities of each individual face.

As a child and teenager, Landy drew continually. Like many
of his peers, he would copy images from books and magazines
as accurately and carefully as he could. 'I did a lot of drawing
between the ages of 16 and 18', he recalls. 'I never went out,
I was a bit of a hermit and just stayed in, and if I wasn't at my
foundation course at Loughton I'd be at home drawing.'
CW

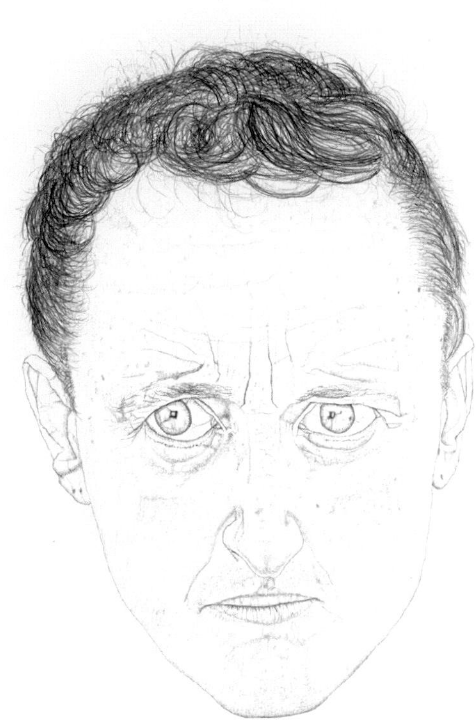

24
Michael Landy
*Untitled (After Cezanne's 'Large Bathers' at the National Gallery, London)*, 2010

Coloured pencil on paper, 28 × 42 cm
Estate of Karsten Schubert, on extended loan to The Whitworth,
The University of Manchester

From 2010 to 2013, Michael Landy was Associate Artist at the National Gallery, London, a period that culminated with the exhibition *Saints Alive*. The Associate Artist scheme was devised as a way of connecting the contemporary world with the gallery's collection of paintings, which range in date from about 1250 to 1900. Until Landy's appointment, all of the previous Associates – among them Paula Rego, Peter Blake and Ana Maria Pacheco – had worked in media that would have been familiar to the Old Masters. This time, however, the gallery chose to invite Landy, an artist whose most well-known and highly celebrated piece was his epic *Break Down* (2001), a remarkable act of destruction and self-denial in which he destroyed everything that he owned, from his passport to his car. Everything was systematically catalogued and then destroyed using an industrial granulator. The whole process took 14 days. In total, 7,227 items were destroyed, bagged up and recycled or sent to landfill.

*Saints Alive* comprised six large-scale kinetic sculptures assembled from assorted junk that was combined with fibreglass representations of various body parts of saints taken from paintings in the National Gallery. When set in motion, the sculptures violently crashed and clattered, scourging themselves with various implements of torture. They were accompanied by a smaller *Saint Francis of Assisi Donation Box*. Every time a coin was dropped in, Saint Francis bashed himself in the face with his crucifix.

Although Landy's sculptures were the main focus of the exhibition, they were complemented by a display of preparatory drawings and collages. Landy's long-term interest in drawing was to provide him with a way into working with the National Gallery collection. His first few weeks in the studio were spent simply looking, and he recalls that he found it fairly hard to conceive what he might do during his two years in residence. He had been encouraged by Peter Blake, who had told him not to worry and that he would know exactly how to proceed as soon as he arrived there. When that did not happen, he felt that he was at something of a loss.

The breakthrough came thanks to Karsten Schubert, who on one of his regular visits to Landy's studio commissioned him to make a drawing from Cézanne's *Bathers* (*Les Grandes Baigneuses*, about 1894–1905, NG6359). Having completed a first version, Landy ended up returning to the painting repeatedly, creating about a dozen responses in total before moving on to make drawings from a small number of other National Gallery paintings. Most of these drawings were to be destroyed by the artist himself and recycled as part of his *Scaled Down* project of 2018, but a small number were rescued by private collectors, including the two shown here.

Drawing from paintings is hardly unconventional, and indeed there is a whole cohort of artists from the preceding generation who have spent many hours drawing from the gallery's collection, including Lucian Freud, Leon Kossoff and Frank Auerbach. It was also an activity undertaken by many of Landy's predecessors as Associate Artists, so Landy was following a well-trodden path. However, in contrast to his artistic predecessors, he chose not to draw in front of the actual painting and instead used a small postcard in the privacy of his studio. Having come to the National Gallery immediately after the completion of his 2010 *Art Bin* project at the South London Gallery, where he had been very much in the public eye, supervising and cataloguing the discarding of failed artworks into a giant purpose-built skip, Landy now felt that he needed to work in private. Consequently, armed with his Cézanne postcard, he locked himself away in the National Gallery studio.

Inevitably, a cheap postcard misrepresents and distorts the original, but this was another reason that led Landy to want to work from it rather than from the original painting. Indeed, Landy's interest in the possibilities of mutilation and destruction as creative acts is something that attracts him to Cézanne's *Bathers*, of which he says, 'I love the way he articulates faces, because he defaces them at the same time.'

CW

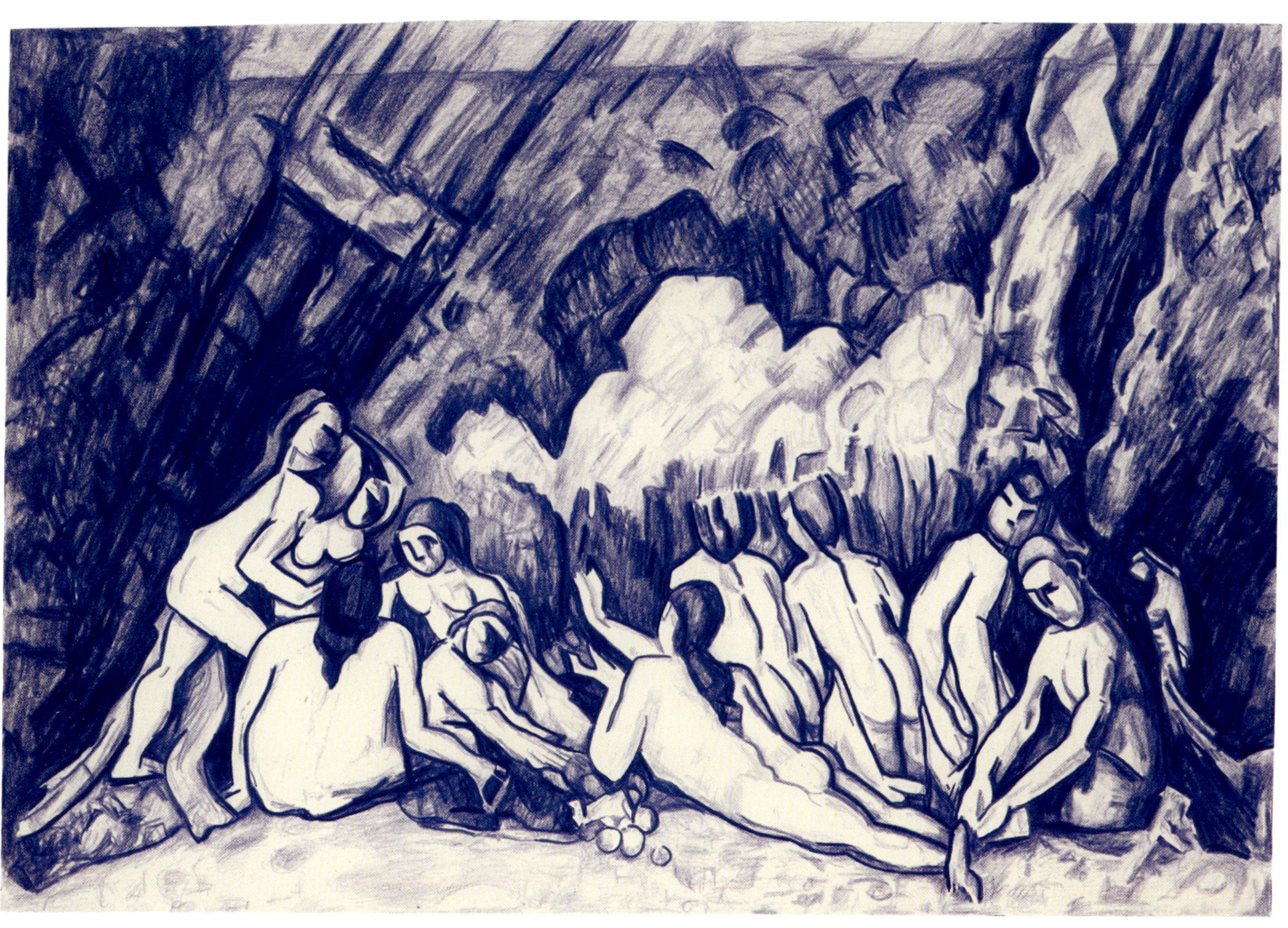

25
Michael Landy
*Untitled (After Cezanne's 'Large Bathers' at the National
Gallery, London)*, 2010

Watercolour pencil on paper, 106.5 × 152 cm
The Whitworth, The University of Manchester, L.2019.7
Karsten Schubert, gift 2019

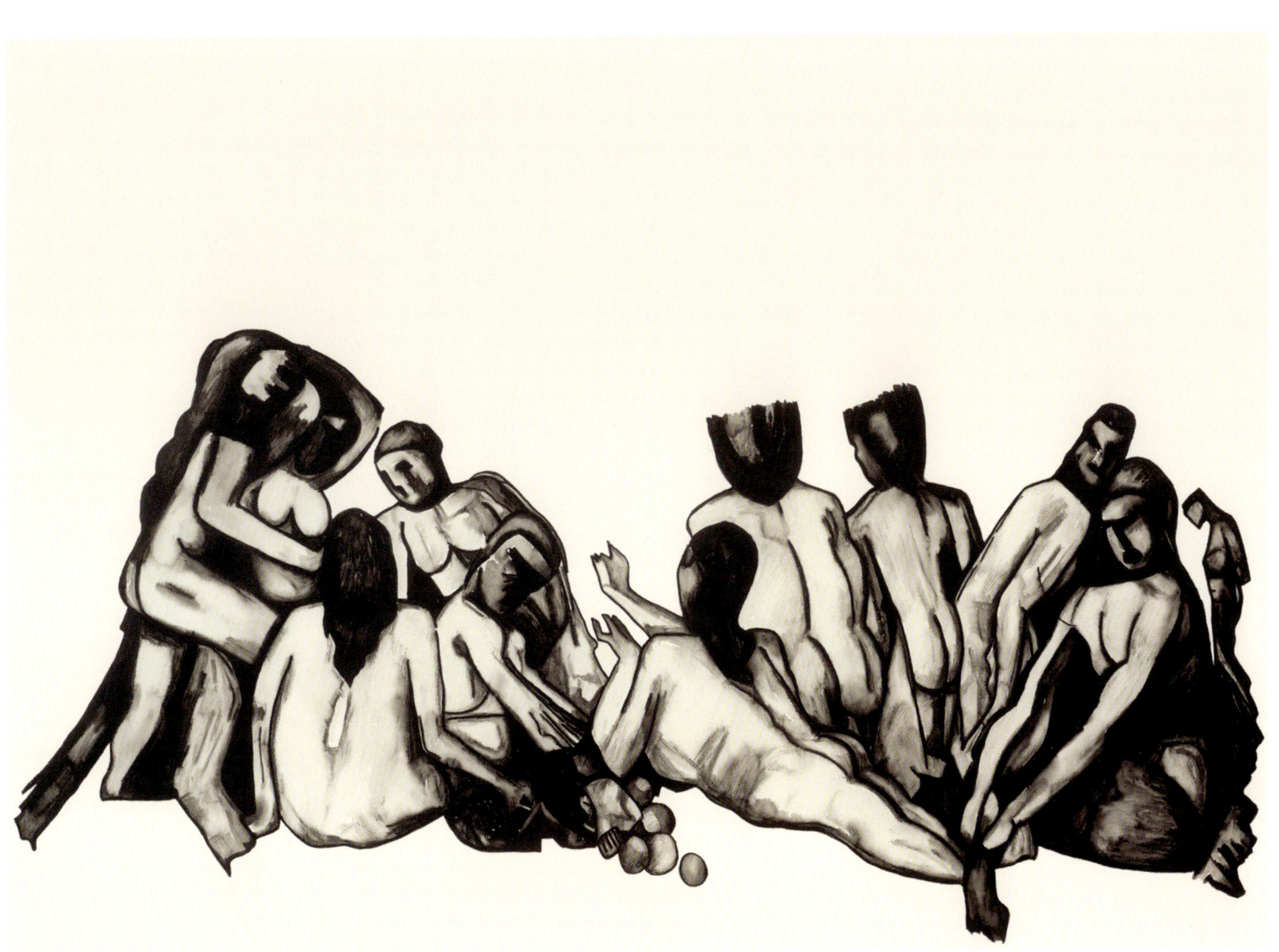

This publication would not have been possible without the generous support of Karsten's many devoted friends. His generosity is reflected in these pages not only through his gift to the Whitworth but also by the many individuals who have helped see his vision through. The deepest of thanks to:

Dawn Ades
Charles Asprey
John Austin
Emanuel von Baeyer
Sarah Barker and Daniel Freeman
Douglas Baxter and Brian Hastings
Madeleine Bertorelli
Lady Madeleine Bessborough
Mel Bochner and Lizbeth Marano
Charles and Leonie Booth-Clibborn
Brian Boylan
Ivor Braka and Kristen McMenamy
Jack Braka
Louisa Buck
François Chantala and Victoria Siddall
Peter Chater and David Hooper
Angela Choon
Martin Clist
Niamh Coghlan
Lynne Cooke
Nicholas Cullinan
Eileen Daley
Thomas Dane
Richard Deacon
Die Keure, Belgium
Caroline Douglas and Guy Morey
Mary Doyle and Kate Macfarlane (Drawing Room)
Rose English
Yuval Etgar
Stephen Feeke
Debbie Fielding
Doro Globus and Gavin Bishop
Lothar Götz
Susanna Heron
Allegra Hicks
John Hilliard
James and Sarah Holland-Hibbert
Richard Hollis and Posy Simmonds
Robert Holyhead and Gemma Lloyd
Ann-Marie James
Tess Jaray
Nicola Kalinsky
Jeremy King

Jack Kirkland
Franz König
Sophie Kullmann
Michael Landy and Gillian Wearing
Glenn Ligon
Simon Linke
Jennifer Lomax
Morgan and Charlie Long
George Loudon
Alma Luxembourg
Caroline Manganaro
Daniel McClean
Keir McGuinness and Dr. Alex Hooi
Jake Miller
John Murphy
Jerome O Drisceoil
Sophie Oppenheimer
Desmond Page and Assun Gelardin
Julian and Felicity Page
Maureen Paley
Dan Perfect and Fiona Rae
Neil Powell
Lady Jill Ritblat OBE
Louisa Robertson (née Green)
Andrea Rose
Tom Rowland
Natalie Rudd
Richard Saltoun
Edwina Sassoon
Nicholas Serota and Teresa Gleadowe
Richard Shone
Lilian Sim
John-Paul Stonard and Katherine Graham
Kostas Synodis
Timothy and Helen Taylor
Mark Thomson
Charis Tyndall (Charles Ede Ltd.)
Robin Vousden
Richard and Jane Wentworth
Sarah Whitfield
Alison Wilding
Paul Winstanley
David Zwirner, London

Published in 2019 by Ridinghouse
and The Whitworth, The University
of Manchester

Accompanies the exhibition
*Cézanne at the Whitworth*
at The Whitworth,
The University of Manchester
Oxford Road
Manchester M15 6ER
24 August 2019 – 1 March 2020

Ridinghouse
46 Lexington Street
London W1F 0LP
United Kingdom
ridinghouse.co.uk

Distributed in the UK and Europe by
Cornerhouse Publications
c/o Home
2 Tony Wilson Place
Manchester M15 4FN
United Kingdom
cornerhousepublications.org

Distributed in the United States and
   Canada by
ARTBOOK | D.A.P.
75 Broad Street, Suite 630
New York, New York 10004
artbook.com

This publication has been made possible
   with Art Fund support

Art Fund_

Texts © Elizabeth Cowling, Yuval Etgar,
Christopher Lloyd, Rosalind McKever,
Richard Shone, Richard Thomson,
Colin Wiggins and Edward Wouk

For the book in this form © Ridinghouse



British Library Cataloguing-in-
   Publication Data
A full catalogue record of this book is
   available from the British Library.

ISBN 978 1 909932 56 2

Ridinghouse Publisher: Sophie Kullmann
Edited by Sophie Kullmann and
   Aimee Selby

Exhibition Curators: Mary Griffiths,
   Samantha Lackey and Karsten Schubert

Designed by Mark Thomson
Set in Lexicon (Bram de Does)

Printed in Belgium by die Keure

Frontispiece: Detail of cat.19:
   Paul Cézanne, *Bathers (Large Plate)*,
   1896–98

Key to catalogue contributors:
EC Elizabeth Cowling
RMCK Rosalind McKever
CW Colin Wiggins
EW Edward Wouk

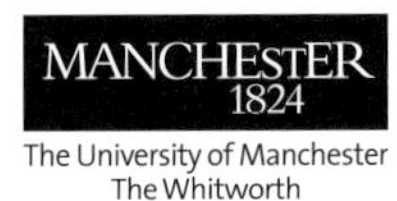

The University of Manchester
The Whitworth

**Ridinghouse**